UNCOMMON SENSE,
COMMON NONSENSE

UNCOMMON SENSE, COMMON NONSENSE

Why some organisations consistently outperform others

Jules Goddard and Tony Eccles

PROFILE BOOKS

This edition published in 2013

First published in Great Britain in 2012 by
Profile Books Ltd
3A Exmouth House
Pine Street
Exmouth Market
London EC1R 0JH
www.profilebooks.com

10 9 8 7 6 5 4

Designed by Sue Lamble
Illustrations by Cherry Goddard

Typeset in Caslon by MacGuru Ltd
info@macguru.org.uk

Printed and bound in Great Britain by
CPI Group (UK) Ltd, Croydon CR0 4YY

A CIP catalogue record for this book is available from the British Library.

ISBN 978 1 84668 602 3
eISBN 978 1 84765 821 0

To my family,
with love

Jules

To Robertson,
my very dear son

Tony

"The day will come when the only battlefields will be markets open to commerce and minds open to ideas." **Victor Hugo**

Contents

Preface to the second edition

OUR AIM IN WRITING THIS BOOK was twofold: we wanted to produce something unusually accessible that would whet the appetites of managers who want to make a difference; and we hoped that our ideas would serve as a catalyst of creative and bold action in an increasingly risk-averse world. The book has already taken hold in companies as diverse as Marriott, Toshiba, Rio Tinto, Roche, Tetra Pak, Deutsche Bank and Zurich.

We believe that most enterprises today are insufficiently entrepreneurial. The thread running through the book is the critical role of imagination and initiative in business. The 67 short sections are written more as a mosaic of ideas and provocations than as a single narrative. There is no right way to read the book; it is intended to be dipped into.

The book is structured around five themes.

Part 1 is about winning

It seeks to define what successful organisations have in common. As part of the answer, it points to the courage to "take the road less travelled", to carve out a distinctive approach to competition, and not to be overawed by the risk of being contrarian. One of the great virtues of markets is that they disproportionately reward firms that have the creativity to see the world differently from their rivals, as well as the courage to act on their unique point of view.

Every competitive industry is, in truth, a creative industry. Yet there is a popular tendency to limit the appellation "creative" to a small number of specialist sectors in a modern economy such as advertising, architecture, design, fashion, film, software, music, publishing and television. By implication, retailing, manufacturing, finance, consulting and education are not creative and have no need of creativity. This is nonsense.

Part 2 is about strategising

It aims to distil the skills required to win competitive battles. Strategic decision-making is modelled as a discovery process. We argue that strategy is less about the **application** of theory than the **activity** of theorising. All too often, however, strategic activity is equated with the drawing up of financial forecasts, the result being that there is an intrinsic bias in favour of efficiency gains and cost-cutting at the expense of revenue growth or marketmaking.

Strategic thinking – putting creativity to work in search of competitive advantage – seems in many organisations to have been captured by the need for elaborate planning rituals. In the majority of companies, for example, strategy can become in thrall to budgeting. If ever there were an example of how a sensible and measured need for bureaucracy had been corrupted to become a tiresome drill of box-ticking and form-filling, it is budgeting – the undisputed champion of managerial nonsense.

Jack Welch expressed the view that "the budget is the bane of corporate America". In Europe, research has found that companies spend an average of 25,000 person days on planning and performance measurement per $1 billion of turnover. And KPMG has shown that the budgeting process takes up 20–30% of managers' and controllers' time. By imprisoning resources over the full length of the planning period, budgeting has the effect of radically reducing a firm's flexibility. Budgeting (and the whole apparatus of negotiating targets and outcomes in a world characterised increasingly by volatility) is a handicapping legacy from an earlier age.

Part 3 is about organising

It focuses particularly on the shortcomings of the standard management model, and the exaggerated faith that, even today, is so often placed in hierarchy and bureaucracy to accomplish the work of motivating and directing human capability. In truth, traditional managerialism is a broken social technology, unfit for the 21st century.

Business has much to learn from organisations such as science laboratories or art schools or symphony orchestras, which take a nobler view of human nature and adopt a less instrumental approach to human talent.

Consider the case of Max Perutz. For more than 30 years from its foundation in 1947, Perutz led the world-famous Laboratory of Molecular Biology in Cambridge, during which time it produced dozens of Fellows of the Royal Society, as well four Nobel prize winners, including Francis Crick and James Watson, the discoverers of the structure of DNA. What set the lab apart was Perutz's inspirational leadership. He understood clearly what brought out the best in creative people and what got in the way: "Creativity in science, as in the arts, cannot be organised", he claimed. "It arises spontaneously from individual talent. Well-run laboratories can foster it, but hierarchical organisation, inflexible, bureaucratic rules, and mountains of futile paperwork can kill it. Discoveries cannot be planned; they pop up, like Puck, in unexpected places."

What is true of science laboratories is just as true, we would claim, of today's business enterprises. Industry, quite as much as science, is deeply reliant upon creativity, and yet the institutional settings in which most companies place their people would strongly suggest otherwise.

Part 4 is about behaving

It adopts the perspective of the individual actor on the corporate stage and how personal influence can be exerted in today's organisations, despite the forces that make this difficult. To work in a typical organisation today is to become subject to pressures and incentives that strongly bias behaviour in particular directions. There are pressures, for example, to play safe, to follow fashion, to procrastinate, to emphasise obstacles, to prioritise the urgent above the important, to play politics, to avoid difficult conversations, to go with the flow, to avoid embarrassment or loss of face, to stay in control, to hold back on emotion, and so on. The problem is that if everyone were to become prey to these pressures, nothing of any strategic significance would ever happen and the organisation would be set up to fail. High-performing organisations rely upon their people – or at least a portion of them – to rise above these conservative and risk-averse forces and, through a kind of far-sighted, enlightened and brave disposition, combine their talents to make a positive difference. These few are the leaders of the organisation, at all levels. We define leadership as the ability to create a culture that can act as a bulwark – a countervailing force – against these biases and as a launch pad for advance.

Part 5 is about learning

It describes a new approach to executive education, managerial development and corporate renewal, based directly upon our ideas about winning, strategising, organising and behaving. This particular form of experiential learning, which we call the Discovery method, grew out of our disenchantment and impatience with didactic programmes taught in lecture theatres in business schools. We describe some vivid corporate examples of the Discovery method in use.

Jules Goddard and Tony Eccles
February 2013

Introduction

....

"Both the ideas that science generates and the way in which science is carried out are entirely counter-intuitive and against common sense."
Lewis Wolpert

THIS IS A BOOK on corporate performance and organisational capability. It puts forward a new explanation for why some companies consistently outperform their rivals; it suggests that beliefs and assumptions rather than goals or values separate winners from losers; it argues that the model of management that prevails in most organisations is both antiquated and harmful; and it proposes a radically different method for how to lead and drive the work of an organisation effectively. It integrates a theory of corporate success with a model of strategic thinking and a method of operational effectiveness.

It is not a textbook. It is more like a handbook of innovative ideas and contrarian perspectives. It challenges the fashion for panaceas, formulae and notions of best practice, and it reflects a view that most business strategies are generic and banal, and most management theories are little more than sophistry or folk wisdom. It seeks to clear away the undergrowth that has made management and strategy far more difficult than they need to be. In a sense, it represents a return to core principles by setting out to reformulate an integrated model of the effective business.

In this endeavour, we seek to engage the creativity of the reader.

Some of the arguments of the book are grounded in recent economic and psychological research, but most of them are the fruit of working closely with executive teams attending management-development programmes at London Business School, INSEAD and elsewhere over the past 25 years. These workshops are hugely revealing of the joys and sorrows of modern managers and the problems they face. This book was written with these managers in mind.

Our approach to competitive strategy derives from a return to economic fundamentals – and, in particular, to the basic law of wealth creation. This is the principle of asymmetric knowledge – that is, any situation when somebody in a market knows something that nobody else in the market knows, and then has the courage to act on that knowledge. We call this type of knowledge "uncommon sense". When such knowledge is acted upon illegally, it is called "insider trading". But when acted upon lawfully, it is called "entrepreneurship". Of course, not just any knowledge will do. It has to be knowledge that can be utilised and packaged in ways that create unique value for buyers. These are the conditions that define the moment of truth that we call "strategic discovery".

In the absence of knowledge asymmetries – and the acts of entrepreneurial courage that turn inert knowledge into incremental wealth – markets would lose their potency. As P.J. O'Rourke, an American satirist, observed:

> If everybody believed what everybody else believed, everybody would set the same price on everything. The middle-aged men on the stock exchange floor could quit hollering and go have lunch.

Markets are battles between belief systems. The winners are those whose beliefs are more grounded in "truth". The beneficiaries are the entrepreneurs and their customers who capture the value embedded in this new knowledge. Market competition is an exploratory process that rewards those who make such discoveries.

As humans we are all fallible. Misconceptions, illusions, blind spots and false beliefs are part of the human condition. When the same sources of error unite all the competitors in a given space, they become what we call "common nonsense". An important aspect of strategy for the individual firm is the skill of identifying such nonsense and discarding it.

Adopting the perspective of a particular firm ("us") competing against other firms ("them"), we can, at the risk of oversimplification, summarise our main argument as follows.

1. As competitors, we differ from each other, knowingly or tacitly, in the beliefs that drive our respective decisions and actions

our belief system

their belief system

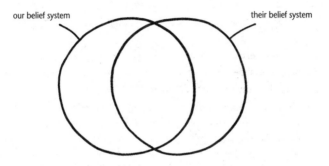

2. Because we inhabit the same reality, most of these beliefs will be shared between us and our competitors

beliefs that
we and they
have in common

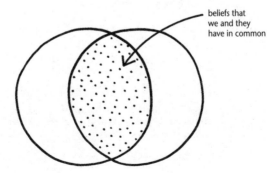

3. Only those beliefs that differentiate us and our competitors, including those beliefs that underpin the skills of implementation, can explain differences of performance between us

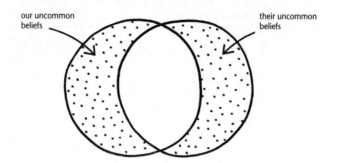

our uncommon beliefs · their uncommon beliefs

4. Winning strategies are based on belief systems that are closer to the truth than those of losing strategies

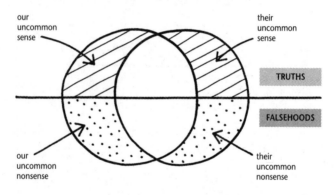

our uncommon sense · their uncommon sense

TRUTHS

FALSEHOODS

our uncommon nonsense · their uncommon nonsense

5. Beliefs that we and our competitors share, whether true or false, cannot be the cause of differential performance between us

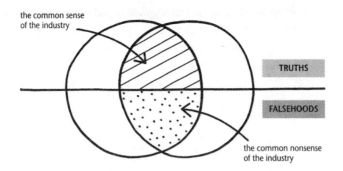

the common sense of the industry

TRUTHS

FALSEHOODS

the common nonsense of the industry

6. Strategising is therefore a discovery process, where the game is won by those who acquire sense and discard nonsense faster than their rivals

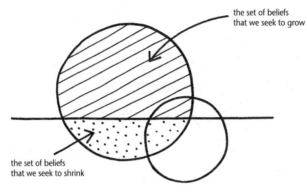

the set of beliefs that we seek to grow

the set of beliefs that we seek to shrink

The standpoints that underpin the arguments in this book can be characterised as supporting:

- the Austrian rather than the neoclassical tradition of microeconomic theory – thus competition is modelled as a discovery process where the rewards flow to entrepreneurs possessing valuable new insights or unique data rather than as a state of equilibrium where the rewards go to those enjoying advantages of scale or experience;

- the assumption that markets are highly imperfect, offering abundant opportunity for discovery, enterprise and differentiation, rather than virtually perfect, demanding no more of management than the dutiful and careful administration of processes and systems;

- the idea that profit is a return on unique practices based on insights drawn from asymmetric market knowledge rather than on best practices based on the theories drawn from economics and social science generally;

- the notion of differentiation, but with reference more to states of knowledge (belief systems, empirical assumptions, statements of fact, mental models, and so on), which vary by truth content, than to forms of ideology (value systems, corporate visions and objectives, statements of intent, end states, and so on), which, if they differ at all, vary only in rhetoric.

Expressed in terms of aphorisms, the book's thesis is that:

- market-based competition is a discovery process;
- asymmetric knowledge is the object of the search;
- the business strategist is the intrepid explorer;
- the effective organisation spurs such exploration.

The demands of management

Business success is both rare and difficult. Indeed, its very rarity argues strongly for just how difficult it actually is. Few companies consistently create significant wealth; over the years, most businesses just "tick over". Yet many management books give an impression that wealth creation is really quite simple – that it is just a matter of following a few principles of common sense and rules of thumb, recipes for success rather like cookbooks.

Creating wealth is subtler than business theory would typically suggest that it is. Common sense is an unreliable guide to good managerial practice. If there is a unifying characteristic of all great business strategies, it is their counter-intuitive character when they are first articulated and executed. (Only much later are they rationalised as being self-evidently sensible.) Writing generic prescriptions for businesses does a huge disservice to the true nature of enterprise and the demanding work done by managers.

In writing about management, it is all too easy to come across as patronising, or opinionated, or facile. In a way, this comes with the territory. Writing such books seems to require an immodest measure of "know-it-all" expertise. We hope we have not fallen prey to these sins. In our view management is one of the most difficult and demanding jobs around.

PART 1

Winners and losers

. . . .

"Dare to think for yourself." **Kant**

MOST THEORIES OF BUSINESS PERFORMANCE rest on the assumption that there is a "right way" to do things. The popularity of notions such as "excellence", "competence" and "best practice" testifies to the hold that this theory has on business managers. Corporate success is treated as a return on doing standard things well.

This may be true of craft skills, such as cookery, pottery and gardening. But it is decidedly not true of any competitive activity, such as sport, warfare or business. In a game of skill, there is no "right way" of playing it. Nor can there ever be a standard way of winning. The point of a game is that it tests a particular kind of intelligence, not the possession of a universal theory or a winning formula. Chess masters do not achieve their mastery through the application of "best practice". They are their own masters.

To have designed a business that creates a sustainable stream of wealth, which is the ultimate test of a successful enterprise, is to have created a singularity. Like a scientific discovery or a work of art, it is a unique, non-repeatable event. It resists generalisation or theoretical explanation. Trying to distil a winning strategy into a universal theory of business success is a doomed, albeit highly fashionable project. It can sometimes be emulated, but that provides no guarantee of comparable success. The winner may well go on winning.

Strategy is the art of first-hand thinking. It deals with one situation at a time. It finds its inspiration in what is unique to that situation. Strategic solutions do not generalise. They are built on insights, not rules or principles. Insights are small-scale, often short-lived discoveries. Something is noticed that had not been seen before. Entrepreneurship, the rare skill of marketmaking, is essentially the skill of producing just such insights and then having the courage and patience to apply them to the design of new products and services. Every great business started life as the embodiment of a particularly powerful insight. Businesses decline as the production of new insights dries up.

A theory of business therefore cannot be a substitute for insight. Any theory that puts forward a winning recipe for commercial success is a fraud. The most it can do is to offer a suggestive method – or heuristic – either for recognising potent insights or for designing conditions conducive to discovering such insights. The same is true of any creative endeavour, whether in science or in art. There cannot be an algorithm for making scientific discoveries or creating artistic masterpieces. The so-called "scientific method" is not a method at all. It merely defines the criteria for what counts as a scientific proposition (such as testability and falsifiability); and it specifies ways of testing the truth of such propositions (such as experimentation). But the act of discovery itself remains immune from all attempts to systematise it.

Business, when it is operating well, is a highly creative activity that works to much the same "logic of discovery" as do science and art. All three bring something new into the world. In science, hypotheses are tested for their fit with reality. In art, paintings, poems and compositions are tested for their ability to stand the test of time. In business, products and services are tested for their profitability in the marketplace.

This book aims to liberate the entrepreneurial imagination in managers by challenging orthodoxy and by proposing thought-provoking heresies.

🌑 Firms outperform their competitors by aiming to be different, not better

Antithesis: the search for excellence

> "Strategy is about setting yourself apart from the competition. It's not a matter of being better at what you do – it's a matter of being different at what you do." **Michael Porter**

> "You don't want to be the best of the best. You want to be the only one who does what you do." **Jerry Garcia**

WINNERS MAKE MARKETS. To make a market means to bring something new into existence. For the customer, it means creating a new category of choice, not simply another variant within an existing class of well-established products or services. Entrepreneurship, which is essentially the skill of combining insights in new ways to make a market, is the dynamic component of a market economy. It is the wellspring of economic development and wealth creation. The entrepreneur identifies these opportunities through a judicious mix of insight and foresight and then brings together the productive resources necessary to capture these opportunities. It is a form of discovery. Albert Szent-Gyorgy, an American biochemist, observed: "Discovery consists in seeing what everybody has seen and thinking what nobody has thought." Every wealth-creating idea begins life as a brave conjecture. Mark Casson, an economist, has argued:

> The entrepreneur believes that he is right, while everyone else is wrong. Thus the essence of entrepreneurship is being different – being different because one has a different perception of the situation. It is this that makes the entrepreneur so important.

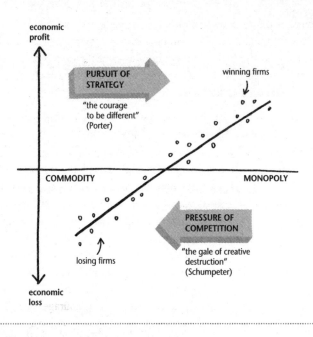

Profit is the reward for daring to be unique

Aiming to be different from competitors does not, of course, guarantee success. All that can be said is that it is the necessary but not sufficient condition of success. Aiming merely to be better than competitors, however, is perilous. While not guaranteeing failure, it has the perverse effect of making competitors more alike, if only because each of them will tend to define "betterness" in identical terms. So the more competitors pursue "betterness", the more they will converge upon the same solutions.

In the modern world the forces of convergence are powerful. To the extent that we see the world alike, we will make decisions alike. And this, of course, defeats the purpose of market competition. It is only through variety of interpretation, diversity of strategy and the testing of these interpretations and decisions in the cauldron of market competition that progress is made and markets justify the "waste" that all experimentation entails. Convergent thinking often leads to the belief that economies of scale are the secret of success – yet scale, like reputation or relative cost advantage, is the result of success, not its cause.

Managers are not paid to make the same decisions as their competitors, however skilful the reasoning that goes into these decisions. Managers are paid to carve out a distinctive approach to the future, to take the risk of being wrong, but at least to give imagination a free rein and the chance to outperform or even defeat competitors. Perversely, the more we try to be logical in our reasoning, and the more we endeavour to base our decisions upon established knowledge, and the closer we adhere to generic principles of strategy, the more likely we are to be driving the business into the middle ground of mediocrity. This is what makes business both frustrating and exciting and what draws intelligent people into it. Success in business rests on the intellectual courage to resist the obvious strategy, to see through the standard version, to go beyond the popular fad, and to steer one's own course. To be too logical is to choose to be part of the herd. And markets do not reward herding behaviour.

Sometimes it is claimed that winners are simply better or faster or more thorough at implementation than their rivals. Every competitor may share the same broad strategic goals, but the different level of skill that they each bring to the achievement of these goals is what separates winners from losers. Yet implementation, no less than strategy, is itself based on a belief system. If implementation is to be the basis of competitive advantage, it will need to be grounded in a set of assumptions that subverts the standard method of implementation. Aiming to be "better at implementation" is no more a recipe for success than aiming to be better generally. The search for excellence is counterproductive. Doing the wrong things right, however well they are done, is inevitably a wealth-destructive practice.

Russell Ackoff, an organisational theorist, observed:

> The righter we do the wrong thing, the wronger we become. Therefore, when we correct a mistake doing the wrong thing we become wronger. It is better to do the right thing wrong than the wrong thing right.

◔ Winning is a singularity, whereas losing conforms to a pattern

Source of error: competitive plagiarism

"The behaviour of peer companies, whether they are expanding, acquiring, setting executive compensation or whatever, will be mindlessly imitated." **Warren Buffett**

WINNERS COME IN TWO VARIETIES: those whose imagination and energy have won them a highly differentiated position in the external markets for customers, for capital or for talent; and those whose inventiveness and perseverance have brought them an equally original approach to the internal challenge of running an efficient operation. Between these two extremes of distinctive products and distinctive processes lie the vast majority of firms. These firms find themselves "stuck in the middle", characterised by me-too products and me-too processes. Differentiated neither externally nor internally, their self-determined fate is to destroy economic value for as long as their strategy amounts to no more than plagiarising the policies and practices of those to either side of them.

It is a rare company that is strongly differentiated both internally and externally. Companies that make extraordinary products are generally run by design engineers whose appreciation of either the importance of profitability and financial prudence or the manufacturability and marketability of their products is secondary to the integrity of the engineering. In the car industry, Porsche has long been an exemplary model of this philosophy. By contrast, companies famous for the leanness of their operations and the

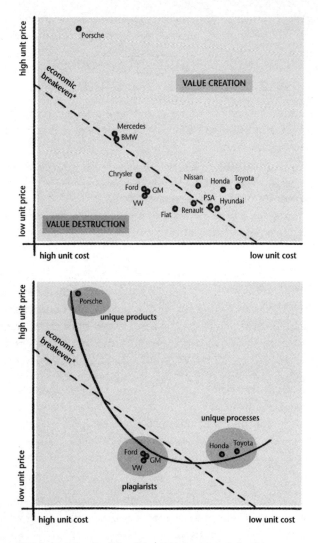

*Long-term return on invested capital = weighted average cost of capital.

Economic profit and loss in the car industry, 2005

The u-shaped profit structure typical of most industries shows two distinctive classes of winners and a single class of losers

Source: Graeme Maxton and John Wormald, *Time for a Model Change*, Cambridge University Press, 2004

persistence of their continuous improvement are typically run by parsimonious manufacturing engineers whose patience for either bleeding-edge technology or fundamental research and blue-sky thinking is equally strained. Toyota brilliantly expresses this philosophy of success.

By contrast, the companies "stuck in the middle" are disproportionately run by self-styled "administrators", whose outlook makes them suspicious of anything parading as entrepreneurial, counter-intuitive, experimental or contrarian. The mantra by which they live is more likely to include the watchwords of compliance, alignment, control and predictability. How often do we hear that companies – and investors – "hate surprises", to which we are tempted to reply, "What, not even good ones?"

The chart shows that markets can be cruel masters. The price of wanting a safe life, at least in business, is the embarrassment of presiding over a failing firm. Paradoxically, many of these faltering businesses, such as General Motors, were themselves once highly distinctive makers of markets. But a loss of nerve at a critical stage in their history – usually associated with the professionalisation of their management and the standardisation of their practices – meant that they slid inexorably into sameness and mediocrity.

⚄ Losers look to competitive benchmarks rather than to their own imagination for their model of success

False trail: the emulation of best practice

"Why are we so often satisfied with 'best practice', when we should be inventing bold new practices?" **Gary Hamel**

"Best practice ≠ best strategy" **McKinsey & Company**

LOSERS FALL VICTIM to the pressures of convergence upon a common set of policies, processes and practices. For managers, it makes sense to play safe. Compared with shareholders, managers have much more at stake in the success of the firm that employs them. This is why managers are more careful with shareholder capital than perhaps shareholders would want them to be. It is rational for senior managers, for example, to take a shorter-term view of the business than their shareholders do. Senior managers are judged more harshly than shareholders for short-term setbacks. This leads to a significant degree of misalignment between principal and agent. It is the single greatest flaw in managerial capitalism. If things go wrong in the business, managers stand to lose their job and a large part of their financial security. By comparison, all that shareholders lose is some value on one of their holdings in a broad portfolio of equities.

It pays for managers to be risk-averse, even if it penalises their shareholders. Playing safe takes many forms: it can mean an excessive concern with compliance, an exaggerated fear of making mistakes, an undue deference to seniority, a disproportionate use

The perils of plagiarism

of consultants as protective cover, an obsession with competitive benchmarking and a bias towards whatever is in fashion. Perhaps the most self-defeating version of conformity, but also paradoxically the safest strategy for the individual executive, is to make "best practice" the gold standard for all decisions and initiatives. The toxic nature of best practice derives from the fact that every competitor in the same market will define "best practice" in startlingly similar terms. So, to the extent that they all track it and chase it, they will effectively commoditise their businesses and thereby forfeit the opportunity to earn economic profit. The concept of best practice is perhaps the single most value-destructive idea to have come out of business schools and management consultancies over the past 20 years. All they have achieved is to urge the laggards to catch up with the herd.

Business is not about best practice. It is about unique practices. Good management permanently guards against anything that threatens to commoditise the business, including anything that encourages the standardisation of thought. To emulate best practice is to abandon any pretence to original thinking. It is simply plagiarism on an industrial scale. Losers, in their search for the failsafe strategy, make the error of believing that success can be made formulaic.

Losers dread failure much more than they covet glory. They would much prefer not to do something that could be the foundation of success than to risk doing something that could go awry. They see success as the absence of error. If you cling to "right first time" as your winning formula, and never take the risk of being "wrong first time", you are taking the greater risk of never learning anything new, never progressing and never experiencing true success. Winners celebrate the mistakes that lead to learning and progress. They do not wait for proof before acting. Losers agonise over every error and setback, however trivial, and waste energy seeking out the culprit.

⊜ Losers define strategy as cost competitiveness and seek efficiency though cost reduction

False trail: the drive for cost leadership

> "Counter-intuitively, managing costs directly causes overall costs to rise, because managers are looking at the wrong thing. If they manage value to the customer, they cause costs to fall – because they are no longer paying to provide what the customer doesn't want."
> **Simon Caulkin**

THE ART OF MANAGEMENT is to manage a business in such a way that the need for operational excellence, continuous improvement, cost leadership, process redesign, cultural change, charismatic leadership or financial incentives becomes redundant and the declared pursuit of these objectives more than any others counts as a clear admission of failure.

When executives reach for these remedies, you can be confident that the business has been mismanaged. There are no surer signs of the inadequacy and delinquency of corporate leadership than that cost efficiency should feature as the dominant issue facing the company, and that the tactics of outsourcing, shared services, reorganisation and other short-term palliatives are being paraded as the main drivers of future profitability. Yet these are the very remedies that most firms "stuck in the middle" choose to adopt.

Strategy is the rare and precious skill of staying one step ahead of the need to be efficient. As soon as such a firm finds itself attracting competitors and pressures on cost start to build, a winning strategy

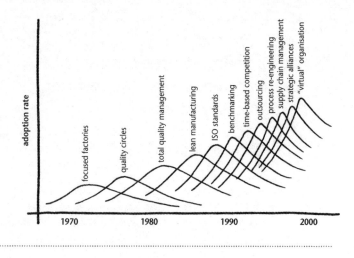

The rise and fall of management fads, fashions and panaceas

will already have been invented to move the business into a new and unassailable market position where demand once again exceeds supply and the firm can continue to be a price-maker, not a price-taker.

The true test of the innovative capability of a firm is that it never needs to worry about, let alone wrestle with, the cost competitiveness of its business model. An example is Apple. Its creativity and courage are of a quality that has immunised it against ever having to resort to such mundane and demoralising activities as operational excellence or change management.

Time devoted to strategies of cost efficiency is simply time stolen from the much more important, difficult and wealth-creative activity of innovation, differentiation and entrepreneurship. Accordingly, the job of accounting is to keep the firm honest to its strategic priorities. Financial accounts should be designed to pick up any signs of commoditisation at the earliest possible stage, before strategic damage is done, for example by detecting any backsliding to policies of "taking cost out" or "downsizing", or indeed any other symptom of a management that has lost its nerve or run out of ideas.

The lead indicators of strategic failure are typically three:

- the firm benchmarks its costs against competitors;
- managers are set targets to close the gap on the most efficient competitor;
- managers seek solutions among the latest management fashions, with the result that the half-life of each new panacea gets shorter and shorter.

Toyota did not get to outperform General Motors by emulating GM practices; it reinvented manufacturing. Yet since 1970, when GM started benchmarking Toyota, GM has sought to recover its lead by emulating the Toyota production system.

The day that Google starts to take an interest in competency profiling or balanced scorecards or corporate social responsibility or some other form of management sophistry is the day to sell Google stock.

Success is best measured by added value, not profit

"Over the past decade the [accounting] profession has completely lost any sense of what accounts are for ... Accounts do not reflect reality. They reflect an extremely complex set of standards comprehensible to a tiny minority of professionals, if that. They are full of weird conventions such as goodwill write-offs, share options accounting and revenue recognition that I defy anyone to call reality ... If accounts reflect reality and accounting standards are just fine, how is it that every bank in the UK has in effect become bankrupt when every single one received a clean audit opinion, including a going concern test [within a year of going broke]?" James Noble FCA

ANY DISCUSSION OF WINNERS AND LOSERS needs a definition of performance that provides a simple and unambiguous criterion for identifying winners. The performance of a business is not measured by its scale, or its growth, or its market share, or its profits, or its return on capital. These all impinge upon performance, but none of them comes close to telling the whole story. The best single measure, and the one that subsumes all the others, is what economists call "rent" and what we shall call "added value".

Business success is proportional to its ability to add value to the resources it uses. These resources include human talent, materials and capital. Added value is the difference between the market value of a firm's outputs and the total cost of its inputs. It measures, in effect, the loss to the economy if the firm were to be expropriated

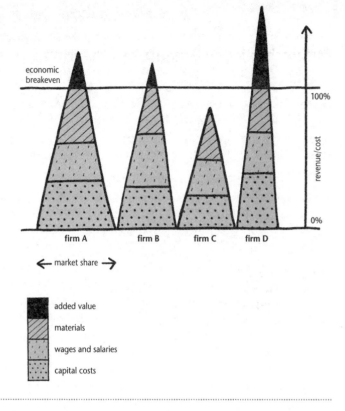

Added value: the true measure of corporate performance

and all its assets lost for use. In this sense, it is the opportunity cost of the firm's very existence.

Added value is less than the operating profit of the firm, the accountant's traditional definition of performance, because it takes account of the cost of capital invested in the business. In this sense, it can be said that the bottom line, as traditionally measured, is not the true bottom line at all.

A business can be very efficient in adding value. In other words, the ratio of its outputs to its inputs is high relative to its competitors. It uses fewer resources to create a given level of sales. This is a good indicator of the competitive advantage created by the business. Alternatively, a business can be very effective in adding value. In this case, the magnitude of the difference between the inputs and the outputs is high relative to its competitors. This is less a measure of competitive advantage than one of relative scale. As a business grows in size and complexity, so its added value typically grows in magnitude but declines in efficiency. Over the life cycle of a business, efficiency is usually exchanged for effectiveness, as focus is sacrificed for scale.

Few companies compute their added value. As a result, the boards of many companies are "flying blind". Because a company's accounting profit is only weakly correlated with its market value, they do not know how well their business is truly performing, with the result that a policy of maximising profit or price/earnings or return on capital can only be perverse and wasteful. Recognising that financial accounts are based on a serious misconception of corporate performance, consulting firms have made many attempts to align accounting methods more closely with sound economic theory and to focus upon measures that are more strongly correlated with shareholder value. For example, Stern Stewart, a management consulting firm, actively promotes the concept of economic value added (EVA), its proprietary alternative to the accounting profession's fixation on profit.

The best benchmark is the competition, not the plan

"The real profit ultimately earned from a business is simply the realisation of relative advantage." **Kenneth Simmonds**

HOW MUCH VALUE does a business need to add for this to count as a success? Performance is always relative – but relative to what? If we are to know whether performance is good or bad, improving or deteriorating, accelerating or decelerating, we need a standard of comparison. So with what benchmark or index should a business compare its results and its added value?

Traditionally, companies compare each year's performance with the previous year's performance. Financial accounts are generally laid out this way. The assumption is that the firm is doing well if the key accounting numbers are moving in the "right direction" – increased sales, lower unit costs, higher productivity, enhanced margins, larger profits, and so on. There are several problems with using the past as the critical benchmark. First, it is an inward-looking measure, with the result that seemingly good results can mask a worsening competitive position if at least some rivals are doing better still – and vice versa. Accounts do not pick up the fact that, by definition, every competitor except one is losing to at least one of its competitors at any stage in the game. In many industries, every player can be led to believe on the basis of their financial accounts that their competitive position is strengthening from year to year. Traditional accounts actively aid and abet this kind of deception.

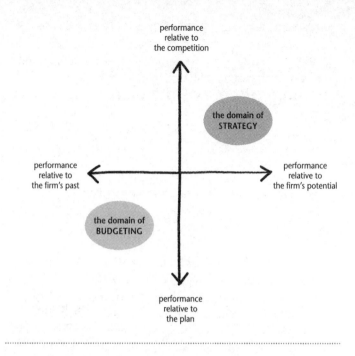

Four contrasting types of performance benchmark

Second, this approach sets the bar rather low. For most companies, particularly in a growing economy and ignoring inflation, beating last year's results is not particularly heroic. As a result, the vast majority of companies use budgets to set a more demanding benchmark, taking into account changing economic circumstances and the declared aspirations of the executive leadership. But this is still an introspective exercise. Beating budget is by no means the same thing as beating competitors. Indeed, it is often observed that budgeting actively rewards managers of business units for aiming low so as to be sure of "making the numbers" and avoiding the embarrassment (or worse) of failing to do so.

For a benchmark to provide a true measure of performance and the right focus of attention, it needs to be externally based. Two such benchmarks suggest themselves: performance relative to key competitors and performance relative to market opportunity or to potential. The latter is particularly difficult to define: opportunity exists only in the mind of the entrepreneurial manager, and is therefore too subjective or too elusive to use as a benchmark. But the former is eminently suitable as a focus for performance. Is the firm winning or losing in relation to its closest competitors? Except where the activity portfolio differs markedly among competitors, one particularly powerful measure is the firm's share of the aggregate economic value added by all the firms competing for the same customers – and how this share is changing. A firm can justifiably be said to be winning if its share of the wealth created by the strategic segment of which it is a member is growing faster than that of its rivals.

The task for accounting is to design and administer financial accounts that track competitive performance. If the accounting function is to contribute to the business it serves, it must be radically re-engineered to place the concept of economic added value at the heart of its measurement system and to use it routinely to track the ebb and flow of competitive position.

Winners are motivated more by meeting a need than a target

Source of error: performance targets

"Don't aim for success – the more you aim at it and make it a target, the more you are going to miss it. For success, like happiness, cannot be pursued; it must ensue, and it only does so as the unintended side-effect of one's dedication to a cause greater than oneself or as the by-product of one's surrender to a person other than oneself. Happiness must happen, and the same holds for success: you have to let it happen by not caring about it." **Victor Frankl**

WINNERS ARE MORE LIKELY to set out to serve than to win. This is a particular case of a general rule, sometimes called the oblique principle. This rule suggests that we do not normally get what we aim for. Companies with purely financial objectives are not as profitable as those with more customer-centred objectives. For example, James Collins, who has researched enduring great companies for some 20 years, found that companies that set out to maximise profits end up being less profitable, on average, than those with more "visionary" goals. Indeed, this "round-about method of thinking" has always been at the heart of the marketing concept: winners discover that the best way to enrich their share-holders is to focus their collective efforts on creating value for their customers. Shareholder returns are, in this sense, a by-product of the ability to create a continuous flow of repeat customers.

Peter Drucker, one of the founders of management as a field of study, famously made the point that "the purpose of a business is to create a customer". Economic profit is the reward that markets bestow on those firms that succeed in this endeavour. In other words, profit may well be the most reliable measure that we have of a company's success – and of course it also provides the fuel for a business to continue to create a sustainable population of repeat customers – but as an objective for the business and as a focus for the activity of its employees, it is counterproductive.

Likewise, the method of thinking that uses anticipated cash flows rather than anticipated competitive market response to judge the viability of any particular strategy is flawed. The focus of investment appraisal should be upon the reasons for believing that one strategy will beat another, not upon ways of configuring the cash flow estimates to yield the right new present value. It is notoriously easier to invent positive cash flows than viable winning strategies. Cash flows are the consequence of strategies, not their justification. Financial markets are fair. A positive net present value is the reward that markets give to firms for competing effectively in customer markets. Cash flow projections merely add a disingenuous element of spurious precision.

The oblique principle also has many other applications in business. For example, financial measures of performance are a lousy way to motivate employees. Most of us do not go to work to enrich shareholders even though we recognise the virtues and merits of capitalism. We go to work to express our talents, to earn a living, to socialise with colleagues, to participate in exciting projects and perhaps to make a difference to the world. Effective organisations play to these motives. Winners seek to fulfil the higher needs of their employees.

⬤ The difference between winners and losers is less their aims and more their methods

Red herrings: vision and mission statements

"When we deliberate, it is about means, not ends." **Aristotle**

A POWERFUL APPLICATION of the oblique principle lies in the finding that goals are better achieved by focusing on the underlying belief system rather than on the goal itself. As the proverb has it: the road to hell is paved with good intentions.

What differentiates firms is not their respective aims and objectives, but their beliefs and assumptions. "What sets us against each other is not our aims – they all come to the same thing – but our methods, which are the fruit of our varied reasoning." This principle, put forward by Antoine de St Exupéry, author of *Le Petit Prince*, builds on Aristotle's observation that men generally agree on what they are seeking to achieve but disagree on how to go about it. The modern fetish for visions, missions, objectives, targets, key performance indicators, milestones, budgets and all forms of promises, intentions and commitments is invariably deployed as a substitute for the much tougher discipline of discovering market insights.

In business, true beliefs deliver much greater wealth than virtuous goals. (It is much the same in politics.) Productive strategic debate focuses on the market assumptions that discriminate between competitors, not on the policies, processes or principles that are simply the expression of these assumptions.

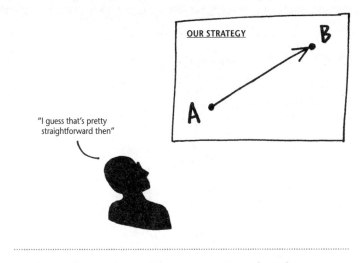

The shortest distance between two points may not always be a straight line

Performance is a return on right beliefs, not right intentions. The choice of strategy is not between outcomes but between means. The creation of economic value makes sense as a firm's goal but not as a firm's strategy. Nor does growth or profitability or market share or any other measure, financial or otherwise, make sense as a strategy. These may well be the outcomes of the strategy, but they are not the inspirational sources of the strategy. The language of strategy typically includes phrases such as cost leadership, or total quality, or market segmentation, or product innovation, or process improvement, or technological leadership, or speed to market, or operating efficiency, or service differentiation. Strategies that jump straight to these generic descriptors of policy without first discovering some new fact about, or insight into, the preferences or behaviours of actual or potential customers simply short-circuit the real work of strategy. Thus strategy is not synonymous with a firm's core competence, or its process architecture, or its scale, or its cost position, or its reputation. These sources of competitive advantage are as much the prized consequence of a winning strategy as its goal.

"We will be a leader of our industry in the future, committed to delivering excellent quality and service to our customers, increasing returns to our shareholders, showing responsibility to the environment, exemplifying the highest ethical standards, and building a highly motivated workforce..."

The universal, all-purpose mission statement

Strategic planners too often assume that the delivery of competitive advantage demands little more of them than a statement of strategic intent or corporate vision, and they dump onto the firm's operating managers the task of turning that aspiration into reality.

❧ The greatest threats to corporate performance are internal, not external

"Companies fall prey to active inertia – responding to even the most disruptive market shifts by accelerating activities that succeeded in the past." **Donald Sull**

"Do not repeat the tactics which have gained you one victory, but let your methods be regulated by the infinite variety of circumstances." **Sun Tzu**

"We are what we repeatedly do." **Aristotle**

GREAT BUSINESSES SURRENDER their leadership position when they become prisoners of their own dogma.

Companies are rarely brought low by external forces. The majority of corporate crises, sometimes called "stall points", when revenue growth slackens dramatically or even reverses, are self-inflicted. The two root causes of stall points are myopia and complacency. Myopia is the failure to recognise market discontinuities until it is too late to respond effectively. Complacency is the belief that the company's strategy is invincible.

Research by the Corporate Strategy Board has shown that uncontrollable factors external to a company – such as regulatory actions, economic downturns, geopolitical events and currency fluctuations – account for fewer than 20% of stall points. For over 80% of them the causes are internal and controllable. It has been said that "companies are rarely killed; they prefer to commit suicide".

Of the controllable factors, the most important are strategic

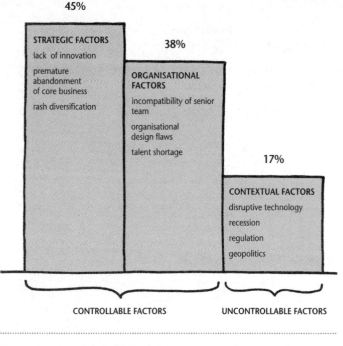

The root causes of stall points

Source: Conference Board

errors, such as the mismanagement of innovation, over-reliance on a dominant position, the premature abandonment of a core business, loss of strategic focus, or neglect of a disruptive technology. Others are organisational failings, such as weak team-working at the top, a poor mix of performance measures, inept processes, or inaction of the board.

From this, we can infer that the greatest threat to performance comes from within the firm and that a large part of performance management should therefore be dedicated to immunising the firm against these internal pathogens. Winston Churchill observed: "War is little more than a catalogue of mistakes and misfortunes." This is a variant of the "cock-up theory of warfare":

- Armies make a cock-up of everything.
- The more they try to do, the greater the chances of a cock-up.
- The best way to win battles is to do nothing and wait for the other lot to cock things up.

Fully recognising the perils of incompetence and error, winners generally look to their own actions and assumptions when things go wrong. They guard particularly against complacency and myopia. By contrast, losers prefer to find excuses and scapegoats for their performance. They are more likely to give a greater role to external forces, blaming such factors as the economy, the populace, the government and the weather when performance dips.

It is better to be first than it is to be better

"It's much easier to get into the mind first than to try to convince someone you have a better product than the one that did get there first." Al Ries and Jack Trout

THE MOST POPULAR EXPLANATION for differing market shares lies in differing levels of quality. The brand leader, so the argument goes, is the one with the best product or service offering, while the brand "followers" are characterised by inferior products and services. The lesson drawn from this supposed correlation is that share is the reward for functional quality (what economists call "utility") and that gaining share from competitors depends essentially upon making credible, evidence-based claims of product improvement. Competition is assumed to be a battle between products along quality lines. The leaders deserve to be leading by virtue of the objective quality built into their offering.

There is scant evidence for this view. Market shares are more reliably explained by order of market entry than by measures of utility. One of the largest corporate-performance studies, the Profit Impact of Marketing Strategy (PIMS) database, supports this line of argument by showing that pioneers have an average market share of 29% in consumer markets compared with the late entrants' 13%. In industrial markets, the numbers are 29% and 15% respectively. In other words, if you had to explain market leadership in terms of a single variable, you would be wise to point to the firm that created the market.

Markets have addictive properties. Once established as the market creator and leader, this position is difficult to dislodge. Markets, like mountains, have a single summit; and buyers have an irrational and enduring bond with the brand that sits on the summit. It usually takes more than technical arguments of superiority to dislodge a leader, particularly if the leader invests in maintaining its reputation for sales supremacy and market dominance. This position is inherently self-reinforcing. In this sense, the brand leader "owns" its market.

Most of us would like to believe that markets are a fair contest in which, at least over the long run, the best product wins out, with equilibrium being the state of affairs where comparative popularity has settled down into becoming a true reflection of comparative quality. Any change in relative quality will change the balance of market shares. But this view would seem to be false. Al Ries and Jack Trout, in their books on the "immutable laws" of marketing and branding, have shown that "it pays to be first":

> Many people think marketing is a battle of products. In the long run, they figure, the best product will win. Marketing people are preoccupied with doing research and "getting the facts". They analyse the situation to make sure that truth is on their side. Then they sail confidently into the marketing arena, secure in the knowledge that they have the best product and that ultimately the best product will win. It's an illusion. There is no objective reality. There are no facts. There are no best products. All that exists in the world of marketing are perceptions in the minds of the customer or prospect. The perception is the reality. Everything else is an illusion.

The practical implication of this line of argument is that it is wasteful to compete for share. Day-to-day rivalry is a misuse of scarce resources. Winning depends upon a rather small number of significant inventions that offer a firm a chance to create and "own" a market and then reap the twin rewards of sales dominance and sales resilience. Yet few marketing budgets reflect this reality.

Most marketing funds are spent on tit-for-tat rivalry rather than pioneering marketmaking.

It is also important to define carefully what is meant by being "first to market" or, in the language of economics, a "first mover". It echoes the important distinction between inventors and innovators. Inventors bring something new into the world; whereas innovators succeed in the rarer and more difficult task of using what is new to solve a problem that is important to people. First-mover advantages do not accrue to those who are first with a new idea or even a new product but to those whose products and services are first to win the approval of users and, in so doing, build a customer franchise. Only the market can determine who is the true first mover.

This is akin to the "fast second" thesis of Constantinos Markides and Paul Geroski, strategy experts and writers, who argue that most market leaders are not those who were first to make available to markets radically new technologies but those who were first to scale up these technologies into mass-marketable products and services. Making a market relies less on the creative skills to be technological pioneers and more on the entrepreneurial skills of translating these new ideas into highly desirable, affordable and available market offerings. Online bookselling, for example, was invented in 1991 by Charles Stack, the owner of a bookshop in Ohio. It was not until 1995 that Amazon entered the market and turned Stack's idea into a mass market. For the purposes of this argument, Amazon, not Stack, is the real first mover. Stack's part in the process was to be merely the "first thinker".

Losers are typified by the "catch up" strategy of "a better product at a lower price"

....

Source of error: blind-paired comparison tests

....

THE VAST MAJORITY OF COMPANIES, when planning for growth, base their marketing strategy on a superior product when benchmarked against the competition. Procter & Gamble calls this strategy, "winning in a white box". Most research departments and most business development activities are dedicated to this kind of rational stratagem. Marketing is then given the job of persuading prospects to change their brand preferences and their buying habits.

There are several problems with this strategy. First, competitive benchmarking is based on the illusion that buyers base their purchases on objective tests of product quality. The reality is that people use a multitude of quality cues other than those of the product itself when forming their buying preferences. Malcolm Gladwell, explaining the marketing disaster attributed to Coca-Cola when they responded to the proven superiority of Pepsi-Cola in blind taste tastes by reformulating their own cola and launching it as "New Coke", put it this way in his book *Blink*:

> It wasn't just that they placed too much emphasis on sip tests. It was that the entire principle of a blind taste test was ridiculous ... Because in the real world, no one ever drinks Coca-Cola blind. We transfer to our sensation of the Coca-Cola taste all of the unconscious associations we have of the brand, the image, the can, and even the unmistakable red of the logo.

Second, buyers are emotionally invested in their historical choices.

They like what they know. They prefer what is familiar to what is unfamiliar and therefore tinged with risk. They like to keep reaffirming the rightness of their original choice ("I've always had a Buick"). It is less a feeling of loyalty to an old familiar brand than comfort with a habit that has served them well.

Third, market followers typically assume that acquiring customers requires beating market leaders. Armed with a better product, they set out to displace the incumbent supplier. They cast the challenge in the form of switching the loyalties of customers, changing their habits, and altering their tastes and preferences. But "brand switching" is a misnomer. Buyers do not "switch" brands as is commonly assumed. They rarely change their allegiance from one favourite brand to another. They "cycle through" a portfolio of three or four acceptable brands within the same category, albeit by giving most of their purchases to their favourite. In other words, what looks like "switching" is really "cycling". People are not loyal to a single brand but to a small repertoire of available brands. More important still, people do not like changing their habits. They are remarkably "loyal" to their portfolio, particularly to their favourite brand within that portfolio, which typically accounts for 75% of their purchases of the category. People generally stay with what they know and stick with what they have.

Coming late into markets and hoping to steal share on the back of "a better product at a lower price" is virtually doomed to failure, even though it could be said to describe 90% of all the competitive strategies in the world. It is rarely a good policy to attempt to steal share from incumbents rather than to make a market in something genuinely new and different. Most market leaders owe their leadership to the fact that they created the market that they now find themselves dominating and defending. The dynamic for which capitalism is justly famous resides less in intercompany rivalry in existing markets and more in the invention of wholly new business models and the obsolescence of whole industries. In other words, strategy is not about attacking or defending market position, but about the making and unmaking of entire markets.

Incompetence explains performance differences better than competence

"I've often felt there might be more to be gained by studying business failures than business successes. In my business, we try to study where people go astray and why things don't work … If my job was to pick a group of ten stocks in the Dow-Jones average that would outperform the average itself, I would probably not start by picking the ten best. Instead, I would try to pick the 10 or 15 worst performers and take them out of the sample and work with the residuals. It's an inversion process. Start out with failure and then engineer its removal."
Warren Buffett

"One does not learn by doing something right. All that one can derive from doing something right is confirmation of what one already knows. This has some value but not as much as what one can learn from identifying and correcting mistakes." **Russell Ackoff**

SUCCESSFUL COMPANIES TYPICALLY OPERATE the kind of inversion process that Warren Buffett, a celebrated fund manager, advocates. Whether consciously or not, they filter out – and immunise themselves against – many forms of insidious error that routinely afflict less successful companies.

There are certain systemic sources of incompetence in companies. First, incompetence comes in more standard varieties than competence and therefore it lends itself more naturally to codification and analysis. In other words, incompetence is more patterned; and therefore it can be defined more easily in terms of a small number of law-like formulations. Second, effective management

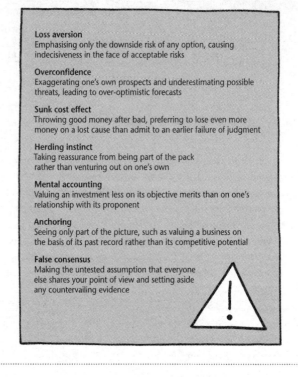

Loss aversion
Emphasising only the downside risk of any option, causing indecisiveness in the face of acceptable risks

Overconfidence
Exaggerating one's own prospects and underestimating possible threats, leading to over-optimistic forecasts

Sunk cost effect
Throwing good money after bad, preferring to lose even more money on a lost cause than admit to an earlier failure of judgment

Herding instinct
Taking reassurance from being part of the pack rather than venturing out on one's own

Mental accounting
Valuing an investment less on its objective merits than on one's relationship with its proponent

Anchoring
Seeing only part of the picture, such as valuing a business on the basis of its past record rather than its competitive potential

False consensus
Making the untested assumption that everyone else shares your point of view and setting aside any countervailing evidence

Seven sources of systemic bias in managerial decision-making

can be defined as the minimisation of mismanagement. In short, good managers avoid the systemic pitfalls, tripwires and errors that, lumped together, we call "organisational incompetence" and "managerial bias".

Incompetence means something much stronger and more toxic than merely the absence of competence; it means a deep seam of counterproductive habits that form an essential part of a company's culture. These habits, often based on mistaken assumptions, particularly about human nature, typically show up in an organisation as misguided policies, maladroit processes and dysfunctional practices. Studies of systemic bias in the perception of risk and the making of decisions, such as those conducted by Amos Tversky, a cognitive and mathematical psychologist, and Daniel Kahneman, a psychologist and Nobel laureate, have shown that managerial judgment is likely to be systematically flawed. Behavioural economists are increasingly demonstrating how our faith in rational choice is generally misplaced.

Incompetence seems to discriminate between companies – and thereby explain performance differences between them – more clearly and dramatically than does competence. In other words, incompetence is a better predictor of corporate failure than competence is of corporate success. Thus, it might be said that management has a greater impact on performance when it reduces the baleful effects of incompetence than when it tries, usually unsuccessfully, to exploit whatever the company identifies as its innate and distinctive competence. In the same vein, Buffett sees failure as intrinsically more interesting and worthy of study than success.

It is important not to confuse incompetence with mere error. Incompetence betrays a certain embeddedness and incorrigibility. As a result, it is not naturally self-correcting or self-limiting. Indeed, this is what sets it apart from concepts such as error, miscalculation, accident, mistake, oversight or slip-up.

When we reflect upon an error, as in the phrase "trial and error", we are more likely to find mistakes that are contingent and temporary. Making mistakes is part and parcel of the fallibility of all human projects. In particular, it is a natural feature of anything experimental in a world as unpredictable as that of business. Its risk is the price of all entrepreneurial endeavour.

The distinction between incompetence and error gives us a definition of mismanagement – and a relatively reliable and straightforward way of recognising it in action. **Mismanagement is the practice of coming down hard on all sources of error in an enterprise while remaining sublimely indifferent to the perils and causes of incompetence**. Put simply, it is the habit of mind that admonishes those who do things that go wrong, while tacitly condoning those who do not do things that could have gone right. This forlorn habit is a reliable recipe for encouraging managers to do as little as possible.

Mismanagement would seem to be a deeper concept than management. First, it is a richer phenomenon in so far as it lends itself more fruitfully to scientific understanding. Success, wherever it occurs, is a singularity; whereas failure clothes itself in a rather small number of generic forms. Second, mismanagement has a disproportionate impact on performance, albeit for the worse. An analogy can be made with the philosophy of morality. Almost all the great moral codes for living well give more weight to vice than to virtue. Seven of the ten Christian commandments take the form "Thou shalt not ...". It is as though the negative concept of sin has more "purchase" on the soul than the positive concept of virtue. Again, Buffett's inversion principle applies. The moral life is marked as much, if not more, by the absence of sin as by the presence of virtue.

🌑 Markets are self-structured to produce few winners and a long tail of losers

Source of error: linear thinking

"Our research shows that in most firms, more than half of all customer accounts are not profitable, and 30% to 40% are only marginally so. It is often a mere 10% to 15% of a company's customer relationships that generate the bulk of its profits." **The MAC Group**

"At the heart of the 80/20 principle is a counter-intuitive yet prevalent fact – the profound imbalance, lopsidedness and lack of correspondence between effort and reward – what scientists call non-linearity. The universe is wonky, yet we still expect an equal ratio of cause to effect." **Richard Koch**

WEALTH IS CREATED by a disproportionately small number of businesses. Only a small proportion of firms are creating the bulk of the world's wealth. The mean rate of return earned by businesses across the world is only sufficient to cover the cost of capital. The distribution pattern of these rates of return is heavily skewed, with the majority of firms failing to earn their cost of capital and only a minority of firms returning value to shareholders. The economic prosperity of the world is disproportionately the result of the skills and efforts of a few strategists in a few companies. Just as 20% of the world's population owns roughly 80% of the world's wealth, so far fewer than 20% are probably responsible for creating more than 80% of its wealth. This is the significance of business strategy.

Most firms are pursuing losing strategies. In any competitive domain, only one strategy, by definition, will be gaining on all the others. Thus, in a domain of ten rivals, there is a 90% chance that

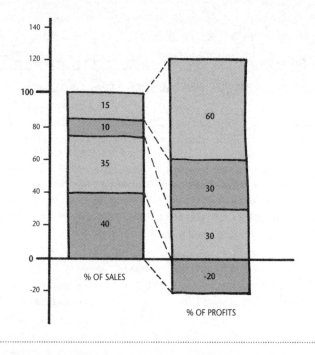

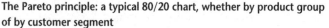

The Pareto principle: a typical 80/20 chart, whether by product group of by customer segment

any one of the ten strategies is losing to at least one other. Since value is being created or destroyed by the quality of the business strategy more than by any other variable under management control, the majority of strategies in play are likely to be destructive of value. Wise strategists acknowledge the frailty of their strategy and the fallibility of their own judgment. They recognise that, more likely than not, they are the author of a losing strategy.

Bias is built into managerial capitalism. As first noted by Vilfredo Pareto, an Italian economist and philosopher, losers in markets dramatically outnumber winners. Economically, 80% of the result, however defined, may come from just 20% of the effort. For example, 80% of a market's revenues, or profits, or growth are likely to be concentrated in 20% of the firms comprising the market. A handful of companies dominate any one of the major industries of the world. Furthermore, within any individual company, whether a winner or a loser, 80% of its value will be concentrated in just 20% of its products, 20% of its customers and 20% of its employees. In other words, much to the consternation of egalitarians, a rather small number of people in the world make all the difference. Most of us are the lucky beneficiaries of this talented minority.

So the first and most obvious explanation for strategic failure is that it is an intrinsic part of the numbers game that we call capitalism. In any game, of course, there has to be a loser. In the "game" of evolution, for example, the distribution of species by population closely resembles the distribution of firms by performance. In markets with numerous players, there will therefore be many losers. But why, it is sometimes asked, is the graph that separates a small number of winners from a large number of losers so steep? How do such seemingly trivial differences in the objective quality of competing products and competing firms get exaggerated to form such dramatic differences in their popularity and success? This, on the face of it, looks unfair. But is it any less fair than the outcome of the evolutionary struggle for survival by species?

⮌ Success is its own multiplier

Misconception: utility as the measure of customer value

"Winner takes all." **Anon**

"Opportunities multiply as they are seized." **Sun Tzu**

IN MARKETS, THERE IS A RELIABLE RULE that "nothing succeeds like success". Buyers treat the popular success of a brand as a clear and unbiased indicator of its true merit. What more trustworthy indicator of value could there possibly be than market acceptance? "A million other buyers can't all be mistaken." And the more that people act on this dubious assumption, the more biased – and seemingly unfair – the distribution of companies and brands by relative performance then becomes. Success begets success. And, just as surely, failure begets failure. This feels unfair because the process is clearly irrational in so far as people are making sweeping judgments on the basis of extremely limited data.

When buyers choose brands, two powerful psychological processes are clearly at work: contagion and habituation. Contagion is the process by which people imitate each other. "I'll have what she's having," as Meg Ryan once said. The more popular something becomes, the more it is endowed with qualities that make it even more popular. Habituation is the process by which we imitate ourselves. We become addicted, so to speak, to what we have tried and found we liked. We are habit-forming creatures. Both of these psychological processes exploit the principle of least effort. When the consequences of making a non-optimal choice between alternative options are trivial, it makes no sense to invest enormous

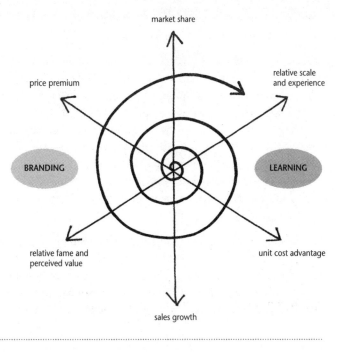

The virtuous spiral of competitive success

effort in making the well-informed choice. Most of the brand choices we make are relatively mundane in the grand scheme of things. Using popularity as a surrogate for quality tends to make for a simpler and less stressful life.

Other surrogate variables include familiarity, notoriety, visibility and availability. Andre Gabor, one of the first behavioural economists, showed that price is used by buyers as an extremely reliable indicator of quality – in contrast to the economist's more traditional view that price is seen simply as the cost of something and carries no other symbolic significance. There is evidence that weight of advertising too is treated by consumers as indicative of intrinsic merit. Experienced buyers, just as much as venture capitalists, are entrepreneurial in the way that they interpret market signals and draw inferences from limited data.

At its worst, contagion can lead to a runaway bandwagon effect, where the link between popularity and intrinsic merit is entirely broken and consumers end up endlessly imitating each other – in a low-level rerun of Dutch tulip mania. Similarly, habit can become dangerously irrational when the "addict" is inhibited from trying anything new or different and the consumer becomes totally brand loyal. In both cases, the buyer is relying on a paucity of data, leading to seriously suboptimal choices. In most markets, however, these sources of irrationality are more than offset by the increasing wealth of information made available to buyers and sellers.

The lesson for strategists is straightforward: many business strategies fail because they rely wholly upon the intrinsic qualities of the product to build market share and neglect the importance of creating the conditions, particularly the perception of the product's popularity, that favour contagion and addiction taking hold.

Most marketing efforts serve only to reinforce the status quo

....

Source of error: market share warfare

....

> "Defining a market is the basis of the segmentation, targeting, and positioning strategies and ultimately of the definition of the marketing mix. Repeated segmentation leads to hyper-fragmentation of markets … these innovation policies do not create new categories or new markets. The innovation always occurs within the category where the idea originated." **Philip Kotler**

THE SYSTEMATICALLY SKEWED DISTRIBUTION of market competitors, whether by sales, market share or financial performance, has been called "natural market structure" by Robert Buzzell, a Harvard Business School marketing professor. It is "natural" on account of both its normality and its innate logic. It is an artefact of certain deep-seated choice processes, such as habituation and contagion.

In most markets, the sales of any one brand relative to the sales of the next larger brand are a constant. This has been called the law of market share proportionality. The average value of the proportionality constant is 67%. In other words, brands are, on average, about two-thirds the size of their next larger competitor. As markets mature, so share differences between competitors diminish (albeit slowly) and so the value of the constant rises with the age of the market. An "average" market with a constant of 0.67 will typically have four major competitors whose shares are roughly 40%, 25%, 15% and 10%. The remaining competitors will share the residual 10%.

The notion of market-share "stickiness" refers to the fact that, once a market settles into such a pattern, the market-share rankings of the leading competitors become remarkably stable. It is rare for any of the top four brands to change position. Why is this?

The short answer is that buying habits die hard. Buyers are predisposed to stay with the brands they know and like. It is partly laziness (sometimes grandly called "the principle of least effort"), partly risk aversion (minimising the economic and psychological "costs" of switching suppliers) and partly cynicism (treating endlessly repeated claims and counter-claims of product superiority with scepticism).

More generally, it is exceedingly difficult to change someone's mind once it is made up. This would be the equivalent of a direct assault on a well-entrenched, well-defended enemy. As in warfare, defending a position is far less expensive than attacking one. It is sometimes claimed that defenders enjoy a 3:1 advantage. In other words, an attacking force, to have an equal chance of victory, would need to be at least three times the size of the defending force. Applying this analogy to markets, it is much cheaper to retain a customer than to win a customer from a competitor. Economic logic would suggest therefore that most marketing effort should go either on sustaining the loyalty of existing customers or on breaking the rules by inventing a wholly new category. Marketing effort is wasted when it goes on predatory tactics in an effort to steal share from competitors.

PART 2

Strategy and tactics

· ·

"There is nothing as useless as doing efficiently that which should not be done at all." **Peter Drucker**

THE PURSUIT OF COMPETITIVE ADVANTAGE can be characterised as a process of corporate individuation. This is stronger than the more conventional notions of market positioning and product differentiation. It reaches deep into the organisation and its self-concept. In psychological literature, individuation is a process of self-actualisation. Applied to the world of business, it implies that success flows to those firms that authentically operate an idiosyncratic, self-discovered and coherent belief system.

The individuation of a business is the expression of two distinctive capabilities: inventiveness (the conjectural process of generating ideas and options) and discovery (the experimental process of testing their feasibility and viability). Yet despite their critical relevance to wealth creation and corporate performance, these twin capabilities are in short supply.

Many of the pressures on companies conspire to crowd out inventiveness and discovery. It is generally recognised that business today is dominated by a combination of relatively mundane strategies and a disproportionate fixation on cost-efficient implementation. Excellence in execution cannot compensate for banality of strategy.

A strategy is not a plan of attack but an idea under study

....

Misconception: a strategy is a route map

....

"The strategist's method is very simply to challenge the prevailing assumptions with a single question: Why?" **Kenichi Ohmae**

"There is always a better strategy than the one you have; you just haven't thought of it yet." **Sir Brian Pitman**

FOR A BUSINESS STRATEGY TO COUNT as truly strategic the competitive moves made by a firm over a period of time need to be based upon a unique system of beliefs. All our actions are the manifestation of our assumptions about the consequences of these actions. Every practice is drenched in theory. All practitioners are theorists even though they may not be able to fully specify the theoretical foundations of the decisions they make or the actions they take. Any theory posits a connection between one set of facts and another. This connection will usually take the form of a cause-effect relationship. If X happens, then Y will follow. Indeed, nearly all theories take the form of "if this, then that" statements.

In business the theories that matter typically come in three varieties: those that predict competitive market response to a company's product and marketing strategies; those that predict employee response to its organisational and managerial strategies; and those that predict how the future will be different. All these theories – and others – underpin (and explain) the decisions and actions of the managers holding these opinions and theories. It could be said that managers are highly rational in making the correct inferences from their beliefs, but that they display less

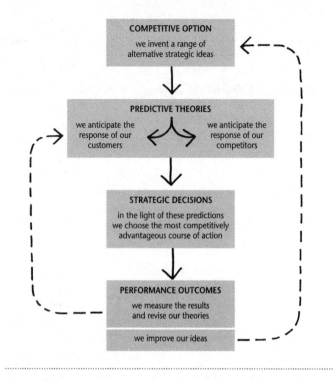

The kernel of any strategy is its model of competitive market response

discipline – and are less rational – in the attention they give to the truth of their theories. In other words, the errors of management are more likely to lie in false belief systems than in fallacious reasoning.

Management is now in a position to set down the minimal conditions for having a strategy. A strategy is a purposive sequence of decisions inferred from a unique belief system or world view. If a business's theories are similar in every key respect to those of its competitors, it is not operating strategically. A strategy is grounded in a difference of view as to how the world works. It is true, of course, that all competitors, however idiosyncratic, will nevertheless share many of the same beliefs, assumptions and suppositions. They inhabit the same world, serve many of the same customers, read the same newspapers and trade journals, commission advice from many of the same consultants, attend the same conferences, and so on. This is to be expected. But competitive success can only be explained by a difference between competitors. And the difference that is most important is a difference of theory, not merely of practice. It is within those elements of belief that differentiate firms that the explanation for success and failure needs to be found. A business does not make money on the beliefs that it shares with its rivals, only on the beliefs that set it apart.

The purpose of planning should be to set out the belief system on which the intended business results will depend. This is not easy. Identifying and exposing the assumptions that underpin actions does not come naturally. But it is only by making tacit assumptions explicit that learning is possible. A bad result can be tracked back to a faulty assumption. A good result serves to corroborate the core assumptions. But what we find in most planning exercises is a rather banal recital of goals and objectives. They are banal because they are truisms. No business sets out to impoverish shareholders, irritate customers, demoralise employees, outrage governments and leave the world worse off – so why write mission statements claiming otherwise?

The measure of a strategy is not its ambition but its truth

Misconception: a strategy is a statement of intent

"Without competitors there would be no need for strategy."
Kenichi Ohmae

"The essence of management is to make knowledge productive." **Peter Drucker**

THE DIFFICULTY OF THINKING STRATEGICALLY is to see the world not only differently but also accurately. Winning strategies are grounded in theories that have greater veracity (or "truth content") than those of rivals. What economists have called asymmetric knowledge, we call "uncommon sense" – "sense" because it is true, and "uncommon" because it belongs only to the winning firm: the winner knows something that its competitors do not know. By contrast, "common nonsense" is the aggregate of all the false assumptions shared by every competitor (including the winning firm).

The theories that inform our actions are inevitably a blend of truths and falsehoods. No one is in possession of the whole truth. What's more, propositions that may once have been true are, as a result of a changing and volatile world, now false. So the ground is forever shifting. Market tastes and preferences change. Technology makes new things possible. What customers once found desirable they no longer do. Thus thoughtfulness, reflection, experimentation and discovery are not options. Just to stand still requires a measure of learning and the acquisition of knowledge. Companies steal ideas from winning firms. Pioneering practices become best

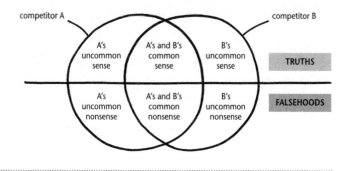

A Venn diagram of the belief systems of two competitors

This shows how each system is a composite of four types of assumption, depending on whether these assumptions are true or false, and shared or unshared

practices, which in turn become standard practices. The playing field is forever being levelled.

What makes a life in business both exciting and frustrating is that we know, so to speak, that half of our beliefs are false, but we are sublimely ignorant of which half. A life in business is a journey of discovery, uncovering falsehoods and formulating new hypotheses. Indeed, the pace of collective learning is a reliable measure of the core capability of the organisation. To be learning faster than competitors is the best indicator and guarantor of strategic success.

Learning is as much a process of purposeful forgetting as of purposive discovery. We need to slough off falsehoods with the same discipline and zeal that we bring to the search for new truths. This effort requires creativity and courage, virtues that sit uncomfortably in many corporate environments. A learning organisation is one that displays high levels of tolerance for mistakes made in the conscientious pursuit of knowledge and truth. In conclusion, the competitiveness of a strategy lies in the truth of the assumptions embedded within it – compared with that of competitors.

The greatest barriers to competition are not structural or economic, but personal or cognitive

Misconception: confidentiality is a barrier to entry

"Incredulity is the wisdom of the fool." **Josh Billings**

ECONOMISTS TYPICALLY EXPLAIN the stickiness of markets and the longevity of the competitive advantages enjoyed by winners in terms of economies of scale, or cumulative experience, or intellectual property rights. This assumes that losers can easily identify the advantages enjoyed by winners but find it difficult to emulate or match the sources of their success.

We want to suggest that the most durable barrier of all is simply incredulity. Winning strategies, at least when first launched, are viewed with disbelief by competitors and observers. They are likely to be seen to be fundamentally flawed – and therefore not worth emulating. An example of such heretical thinking was Pilkington's invention of float glass. Only when it is too late to be easily and effectively plagiarised does the wisdom behind the strategy finally dawn.

Imagine the following experiment. All the firms in the same competitive space are invited to share and read each other's five-year strategic plans. As senior executives mull over their rivals' future strategies, they put a tick against all the propositions, policies, processes and practices with which they agree, but a cross against those that strike them as absurd, or perilous, or simply mistaken. The expectation is that there will be far more ticks than crosses on all the plans. In other words, the strategies in any industry dramatically overlap. Companies gravitate towards a broad strategic consensus. The crosses, however, will highlight the views and opinions that divide them. It is the accuracy of these asymmetric assumptions that best explains relative performance and it is the incredulity to which they give rise that best protects each firm's competitive position. Companies imitate only those features of their competitors that they find credible, sagacious and proven. They see no value in stealing those competitive goods that they perceive to be damaged or suspect.

One of the implications of this theory is that confidentiality of corporate strategy is a waste of effort. Winning strategies are best protected by their own heretical status.

Wealth-creating actions are driven more by curiosity than by targets

Misconception: good strategies are more often purposeful than emergent

"Curiosity is the 'open sesame' to learning, even for managers." **Russell Ackoff**

THE ACTIONS THAT, STRUNG TOGETHER over time, create a winning streak, we will call tactics. Tactics are moves in a game that cumulatively builds wealth. Often only much later, long after the decisions were made, can these points of action be connected to tell a coherent story. At the time, these same tactics may well have appeared to the tacticians themselves to be no more than isolated stabs in the dark, reactions to surprising events, or expedient decisions.

Drawing upon the earlier notion of asymmetric knowledge as the wellspring of wealth creation, tactics can be said to come in four varieties of learning. There are moves that contribute to uncommon sense – a form of discovery process; there are moves that recognise uncommon nonsense for what it is and discard it as a misconception – a kind of wilful forgetting. There are moves that "steal" the uncommon sense of competitors and turn it into common sense – a kind of theft or mimetic learning. And there are moves that see through the common nonsense of the industry and, in recognising it as popular mythology, discard it, thereby "parking" these falsehoods exclusively with competitors – a kind of liberation or escape from dogma and superstition.

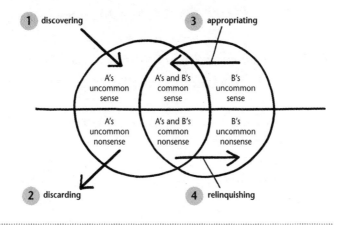

Wealth-creating activities: four varieties of tactical moves

One way of thinking about everyday managerial activity is as a process of knowledge management. Only if the moves in the game take one of these four forms of organisational learning are they contributing to wealth. Naturally, at the time that these moves are made, they are speculative. Only with time, if ever, is it possible to determine their value. In other words, tactical choices are always experiments, at least in the informal sense of the term. They are tentative trials that, in the manner of mutation and selection in the evolutionary process, survive or perish depending upon the impartial judgment of the market. A move that has the potential to create wealth will never be foolproof. It will have a conjectural element. It will "go beyond" the prevailing state of knowledge. Decisions based on evidential proof will only rarely create wealth because such knowledge will usually be in the public domain.

ve strategy is as likely to flow
action as to lead to action

Misconception: rationality means thinking our way
into action rather than acting our way into thought

"People walk in order to find what is worth talking about." **Karl Weick,**
"Talk the Walk"

WHICH COMES FIRST – thought or action? Do we think in
order to organise our actions? Or do we act in order to clarify our
thoughts? It is conventional – but also dangerous – to draw a sharp
distinction between strategy and tactics, between walk and talk,
between formulation and implementation, and between thinking
and doing.

First, there is a widespread belief that each pair is separable into
two distinct activities. Second, it is assumed that the first term of
the pair is the logical antecedent of the second term. For example,
strategy is assumed to precede tactics. The formulation of a plan
precedes its execution. Thought precedes action. Third, each of
the two activities is assigned to two separate groups of people.
For example, those who formulate a strategy are expected to be
different from those who are given the task of implementing it.
And fourth, this separation of roles is overlaid with a hierarchy.
Strategists, formulators and thinkers are normally more senior
than tacticians, implementers and doers.

These four conventional perspectives help to explain why implementation is so often regarded as difficult, contentious and (when
things go wrong) culpable.

Thinking
so as to do

Doing
so as to think

Which comes first: The thought or the deed? The hypothesis or the experiment? The aim or the method?

If implementation is defined as the execution by one group of people of a plan drawn up by another set of people, then it is doomed. If strategy is defined as a set of top-down targets designed to stretch the talents of those further down the organisation, then it too is fated to fail. In prosecuting a strategy, thought and action are entwined. We act in order to test, sort and clarify our thoughts, and we think in order to structure, co-ordinate and direct our actions. There can be no significant distinction between the intention, the idea and the action.

Richard Rumelt, a corporate strategy expert, said in *McKinsey Quarterly* (December 2008):

> By strategy, I mean a cohesive response to a challenge. A real strategy is neither a document nor a forecast but rather an overall approach based on a diagnosis of a challenge. The most important element of a strategy is a coherent viewpoint about the forces at work, not a plan.

Strategies "emerge". They are as much the outcome of spontaneous and improvised action as its source and inspiration. Strategies, then, only make sense in retrospect. We connect the dots and discern a pattern. We call this pattern a strategy – "the result of human action, but not of human design", to borrow a famous phrase from David Hume, a philosopher.

⊜ Strategy belongs more naturally to the crowd than to the professional

Misconception: strategy, like chiropody or dentistry, calls for expertise

"One of the most consistent findings in the literature on decision-making and performance is that the best groups perform better than the best individuals, because groups are able to take advantage of the collective wisdom and insight of multiple individuals, while individual judgments reflect the narrower insights and skills of just one person."
Jeffrey Pfeffer and Robert Sutton

TO THINK OF STRATEGY as just another job is to commit a category mistake. Strategy is not like dentistry or carpentry or playing the French horn, all of them occupations for which technical expertise is necessary. Strategy cannot be delegated to an individual or to a connoisseur of the subject or to an expert. It is not a profession or a craft or an accredited skill. Nor can it be delegated to a committee on behalf of the host organisation, or be left to chance or simply be allowed to happen.

The practice of strategy is more akin to the practice of resource allocation in a market economy. No single person directs the activity, but resources nevertheless get allocated in highly efficient ways to those activities that make best use of them. In other words, strategy is a process by which collective decisions get made without the need for a master designer or a hierarchy of any kind. Markets deliver value because prices convey information that exceeds the knowledge of any single individual. For a firm to be strategically astute, it is equally important that a method is found for aggregating the information that is dispersed among many minds within the organisation.

One such method is a prediction market, or indeed any betting market. For example, the Iowa Electronic Market (IEM) is an online, unregulated futures market where contract pay-offs are based upon real-world events such as political elections, companies' results and stock-price returns. The market is operated by the University of Iowa Business School as an educational and research project. The participants play with real money. Trading accounts can be opened for $5–500. Participants then use their funds to buy and sell contracts. Traders therefore have the opportunity to profit from their trades but must also bear the risk of losing money.

The premise behind the IEM, which became famous for predicting the outcome of the 1988 American presidential election with greater accuracy than any of the national polls, is that voters have no incentive to tell pollsters the truth, whereas when their own money is on the line, they will be far more conscientious in taking into account all the relevant information they can find. Steven Feinstein, a professor at Boston University's School of Management, points out:

> There is a strong incentive for players in these political markets to process information about the candidates and their conclusions are revealed to us through the markets' prices. The IEM works on the same principle as any futures market.

The success of predictive markets in politics has lessons for business. It suggests that when prophecies are being made for which there is little scientific evidence, the surest way of establishing the odds of success for any given strategic option might be to rely on "crowd wisdom", or what Tom Malone, a professor at MIT Sloan School of Management, calls "collective intelligence", rather than so-called "business acumen" or "marketing expertise".

The true strategist resembles an experimental scientist rather than a clairvoyant planner

Misconception: strategy is the application of foresight

"The future is best dealt with using assumptions rather than forecasts."
Russell Ackoff

"Little by little does the trick." **Aesop**

IF CORPORATE SUCCESS in competitive markets is a return on uncommon sense (or asymmetric knowledge), then the process of strategic thinking is akin to the process of scientific discovery. Through conjecture and refutation, a phrase of Karl Popper, a philosopher of science, a firm builds both its proprietary knowledge base and its capacity to create wealth. But can we be more specific than "conjecture and refutation" in the description of this method?

The search is not for law-like relationships or systemic patterns in the external world, which is the normal way of defining the aims of science. It is for the discovery of new facts, temporary patterns and counter-intuitive insights. The result of the search will be singularities rather than generalisations or universal truths. Firms can build a position of strength on a particular combination of tentative and fleeting insights so long as their competitors do not see the world in quite this way.

The process, to the extent that it can be formalised, begins with an element of surprise and the natural curiosity that this arouses

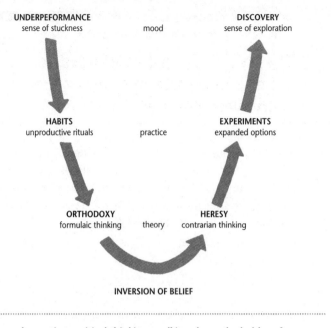

| UNDERPEFORMANCE | | DISCOVERY |
| sense of stuckness | mood | sense of exploration |

| HABITS | | EXPERIMENTS |
| unproductive rituals | practice | expanded options |

| ORTHODOXY | | HERESY |
| formulaic thinking | theory | contrarian thinking |

INVERSION OF BELIEF

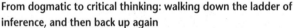

From dogmatic to critical thinking: walking down the ladder of inference, and then back up again

in an open mind. Surprise comes about when the predictions of a cherished theory are found to be false. At this point, strategists recognise that the market is telling them to adjust their theory, however reliable it may have been in the past. A market opportunity has been missed that other firms identified and exploited. Why was this? What set of assumptions blinded the firm to this opportunity? Or an action was taken that turned out to have disastrous results. How come? What set of beliefs led managers astray? In short, the habits and rituals that in the past may have served the firm well are now leading it into error.

Symptoms of underperformance usually betray practices that are counterproductive. At this stage it may be tempting to abandon the process and put another in its place, from whatever source. But this would be simply to treat the symptoms or to chase the latest fashion. The true strategist tries to deconstruct the offending practice into its component assumptions and to question which of these is most likely to be the culprit. In other words, whatever takes the firm by surprise becomes the pretext for a rational process of inquiry. The next step will be to invert these beliefs and state them as testable propositions. In short, the method of discovery involves walking down the ladder of inference – from symptoms of underperformance such as surprise, through practices that are spawning these symptoms, to belief systems that are informing these practices – and then walking back up the ladder, starting with a set of contrarian beliefs, embodying them in business practices and processes, and finally testing the results of these new ideas and ways of working in the marketplace.

There cannot be a method of strategy just as there cannot be a method of science

....

Misconception: there is a right way to "do strategy"

....

"Unhappy the general who comes on the field of battle with a system."
Napoleon

"The real challenge in crafting strategy lies in detecting subtle discontinuities that may undermine a business in the future. And for that there is no technique, no programme, just a sharp mind in touch with the situation." **Henry Mintzberg**

EFFECTIVE STRATEGY ABHORS RULES and formulae. There can be no such thing as an algorithm for formulating a winning strategy in a competitive market. Strategic thinking deals in singularities – with what is unique to a situation or non-recurrent in an event. Effective strategies are provisional, ad hoc and contingent. They are as varied, as fleeting and as idiosyncratic as the market situations for which they are designed. No rule could have generated the strategies that enabled Dell to beat Compaq, or Tesco to beat Sainsbury's, or Google to beat Yahoo, or Rolls-Royce to beat Pratt & Whitney, or Facebook to beat MySpace.

The notion of a "generic strategy" is a contradiction in terms. Just as there can be no such thing as a typical market, or a typical industry, or a typical company or a typical customer, so there can be no such thing as a standard strategy drawn from a pattern book. This is a version of the law of requisite variety: for a strategy to succeed, it must possess something of the same complexity as the competitive environment to which it is fitted. Yet most strategy texts are written as self-help guides, full of homilies and simple rules of success. Armchair strategists cannot resist the temptation to formulate a "methodology" of strategic management. Yet real strategic thinking starts, not with a universal theory, but with a particular problem situation – for example, a set of dilemmas arising from a competitive threat, or a customer complaint, or a market opportunity, or a research finding, or an unexpected happening, or a price move, or a technological breakthrough, or a change of regulation.

A "theory of business" can only describe the average case; whereas strategic thinking, by definition, is the skill of beating the average.

Peter Drucker has observed that the most important and least risky source of innovation is the unexpected event. Whenever we are surprised by events, nature is letting us know that one of our cherished beliefs is false. The entrepreneur hears this quiet voice of dissonance, amplifies it into a business opportunity, draws the entrepreneurial conclusion and acts upon it.

Effective strategic thinking emulates the logic of scientific discovery. Strategy should not adhere, as is often suggested, to an inductive process for getting to ideas, starting with observation, data gathering and statistical analysis, and leading to conclusions. Rather, the sequence of activities should conform to the method of science, starting with problems and questions, then looking for tentative options and answers, and then testing these ideas, from which further, richer problems and questions arise. The worst places to start strategic inquiry are with a generic theory (for example, "never start a price war" or "the cost leader always wins" or "stockmarkets heavily discount conglomerates") or with a "macro-picture" (for example, the future state of the economy, or the size of the potential market, or the emerging forces in the industry). Winning strategies are rarely constructed from knowledge that is widely available in the public domain.

◈ Plans deliver greater value if they are propositions to be tested rather than commitments to be met

••

Misconception: the annual planning cycle is strategy in action

••

"People like to think that businesses are built of numbers (as in the 'bottom line'), or forces (as in 'market forces'), or even flesh and blood ('our people'). But this is wrong. Businesses are made of ideas – ideas expressed in words." **James Champy**

IN MANY COMPANIES, the strategic process has become the home of "thoughting" rather than the catalyst for creative thinking and entrepreneurial endeavour. The problem is that much of what passes for a "strategy" in many firms is little more than a complex edifice of targets and performance indicators. By practising strategy in this way, it has become an unwitting accomplice in the commoditisation of the business. Three particular misconceptions of strategy lie at the heart of this predicament:

● Strategic thinking is seen as synonymous with planning. As a result, strategy has been folded into the financial planning system, with the consequence that:
  – it operates to a periodic, typically annual cycle;
  – its work is done when the plan is filed;
  – its output is little more than an extrapolation of financial forecasts;
  – it becomes contaminated by the politics of the budgeting process;

– it adopts a defensive mentality.

● Strategic insight is assumed to derive from the analysis of data, in particular, market research data. As a result, strategy has fallen prey to what Clay Christiansen, a professor at Harvard Business School, has called, "the innovator's dilemma", meaning that:

– it is driven by customers' (highly unreliable) conceptions of their own future desires and preferences;

– it surrenders itself to retrospective marketing research techniques, such as focus groups, customer surveys and panel data;

– it lacks a competitive dimension;

– it becomes a conservative force in the company.

● Strategic effectiveness is defined as the creation of a perfectly aligned organisation. Everything is optimised for the delivery of arbitrarily established targets, with the result that:

– it becomes consumed with the task of implementation;

– it is judged wholly in terms of meeting published expectations;

– it leaves no room for the redundancy and slack upon which innovation thrives;

– it neglects effectiveness for the sake of efficiency.

Compare these two views of strategy:

● **Definition 1.** A strategy is a choreographed plan of tactical moves made with the express aim of getting to a chosen financial outcome and calibrated against a carefully defined set of performance indicators and organisational commitments. Planning and implementing is the best method for aligning and motivating large numbers of employees in the service of a common purpose. The twin enemies of strategy are disorder and indolence.

● **Definition 2.** A strategy is a sequence of improvised actions taken with the express aim of winning against a chosen set of competitors and grounded in a distinctive set of assumptions about how customers make choices. Testing and learning is the surest way of harnessing the natural curiosity of employees in the cause of new and better ways of competing. The twin enemies of strategy are complacency and myopia.

If, as business strategists, we decided to change the way we practise strategy from the first definition, where we would expect to find ourselves among the vast majority of our peers, to the second definition, where we might feel lonelier and more exposed, we would be committing ourselves to at least three significant changes of focus:

● from the annual plans we make to the everyday actions we take;

● from the customers we serve to the competitors we target;

● from the performance goals we set to the market assumptions we make.

Some practical consequences would follow from this threefold shift of focus. We would:

● operate with an eye to beating competitors rather than beating the budget;

● measure our performance relative to particular competitors rather than to arbitrary targets or to past performance;

● set our objectives in terms of competitive position rather than financial result;

● organise for purposes of experimentation and learning rather than alignment and reward;

● judge our performance in terms of new insights and discoveries rather than pre-set targets and variances;

- select the customers we most wanted to serve on the basis of the competitors we most wanted to beat, rather than vice versa;
- trust the capital markets rather than our own clairvoyance to price the market value of our business – and its component projects and options – accurately and fairly.

Strategic breakthroughs are more likely to arise from adhocracy than a formal planning process

Misconception: the best decisions are based on the strongest evidence

"If your organisation chart 'makes perfect sense', then you probably don't have a particularly innovative enterprise. Adhocracy requires letting go of assumptions of linearity – substituting curves and spirals and Jackson Pollock-like tangles for straight lines and 90-degree turns."
Tom Peters

DAVID OGILVY, an advertising executive and a great believer in "big ideas" in business, thought that the mark of a truly big idea is that it draws the response: "I wish I had thought of that." This may be true of ideas in advertising, but in strategy the big idea is likely to be greeted with exactly the opposite response: "Who could possibly believe in that?" "Whoever came up with that nonsensical idea?"

Strategic ideas, because they are generally contrarian, invite incredulity when first expressed. Only much later, if the idea works, does everyone claim to have always been a fan. "Success has many fathers, while failure is a orphan."

When Collett, Dickenson, Pearce (CDP), a British advertising agency, realised that its most famous and effective advertising campaigns were typically those that had failed most lamentably in research, it decided as a matter of policy to make this a condition for recommending all future advertisements to its clients. CDP's

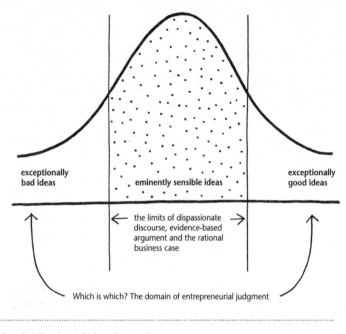

The following labels appear within and around the figure:

exceptionally bad ideas

eminently sensible ideas

exceptionally good ideas

← the limits of dispassionate discourse, evidence-based argument and the rational business case →

Which is which? The domain of entrepreneurial judgment

The distribution of ideas by quality

argument was that advertisements that excelled in research were just the kind of run-of-the-mill, competently made, utterly predictable ads that all its competitors were confidently creating, and that advertisements that bombed in research were either truly dreadful and ineffective or genuinely inspired and ahead of their time. If the client were to express reservations – "How can you be so sure that it has failed in research because it is so good rather than because it is so bad?" – the advertising agency would respond: "That is the judgment that you pay us to make."

The vital signs of a strategically driven business are that it is willing to take these CDP-like risks, go "beyond the research", make judgments "in excess of the facts", give over part of the business to pure experimentation, and recognise that strategy is, in part, a process of trial and error. Strategy is inherently exploratory. If an infallible business case were required to justify every business decision, then strategic innovation would dry up and growth would grind to a halt.

A strategic business casts its net wide. It encourages everyone to have ideas, to be part of the great experiment that any good business aspires to be, and to be welcoming of diverse and contrarian ideas. If people are not making enough brave and ingenious mistakes, concern will be expressed that perhaps they are asleep on the job, or have lost their zest for learning, or are not thinking strategically enough. The prevailing concern will be that market opportunities are being lost by being too risk-averse.

Accordingly, innovators have a high tolerance for failures, even waste. They recognise that there has to be redundancy or surplus capacity in the system in order to create enough surviving innovations to satisfy the company's prosperity-seeking needs. Sumantra Ghoshal, a professor at London Business School and INSEAD, estimated the optimal amount of slack to be about 10% of sales.

At the edge of chaos, mistakes are made. Not every judgment will be sound. Except for those rare firms dedicated to just one transfixing prospect, a would-be innovating organisation needs a pipeline of possibilities, just as in nature. The sea turtle does not lay just one egg.

Business is no different. For a company to survive and prosper through innovation, it has no choice but to place multiple bets. There must be a pipeline of experiments, many of which may be small, needing few resources and perhaps opening up quite limited market opportunities if they succeed. Others may be the equivalent of taking out an option that can be exercised at some time in the future. One reason that big companies have neglected this practice is that most embryonic ideas are simply too small at the initiation stage to grab their attention. This has led to the "scavenging model", where entrepreneurs acquire these languishing ideas from large corporations, rather like scavenger fish cleaning out the mouths of bigger fish.

Theoretically, large companies have a huge advantage over smaller ones when it comes to making a success of innovation. Typically, the entrepreneurial start-up will have sufficient funds to invest in just a single idea. It is hoping that its focus, dedication and energy will more than compensate for taking such a risk. Large companies, by contrast, have the resources, and hence the luxury, of being able to place multiple bets and manage pipelines of possibilities. The pharmaceutical industry is a classic example. More than any other industry, perhaps, it understands the importance of "inefficiency" to innovation. In other industries, the "bias to efficiency" would have firms minimising the number of failures, penalising the makers of mistakes, restricting investment funds to sure-fire successes, disinvesting in anything that looks like a "bet" or an "option" and, above all, reducing "slack" to the bare minimum – all in the cause of profitability.

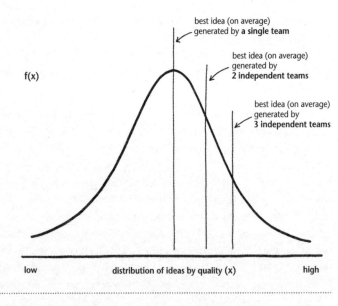

The virtue of replication

Against this narrow and self-defeating notion of efficiency, Irwin Gross, a professor of marketing at the Wharton School, has shown empirically that in advertising, for example, it is more profitable to fund three independent agencies or non-conferring teams to develop and test three competing advertising campaigns in response to a given client brief than to give the job to a single team in the traditional manner. Triplication of effort, while seemingly wasteful, is the most profitable solution in the long run: the best of three independently generated ideas will generally outperform the "best of one" by an amount that exceeds the cost of two extra teams.

◉ Our understanding of strategy owes more to capital markets than to product markets

Misconception: markets for goods and services operate to a different logic from capital markets

"Understanding how to be a good investor makes you a better business manager, and vice versa." **Charlie Munger**

THEORISING ABOUT STRATEGY is bedevilled by the difficulty of isolating strategic factors as the causes of corporate success or failure. The market, it is true, is a perpetual experiment, but the lack of structured experimental design and of control groups makes it difficult to know whether a highly successful firm owes its success to its strategy rather than to some other, non-strategic factor, whether of its own making or not. The question then is: are there any markets that come close to the conditions of a laboratory for testing strategy as a cause of success?

The stockmarket is such a market. First, it is an efficient market where sustainable returns at levels higher than the market as a whole have been shown to be rare. If we could find an investor who had consistently beaten this highly efficient market, we might be closer to finding techniques of thinking or patterns of behaviour that contribute to success and that could be imported into less efficient markets, such as customer or talent markets. After all, it is under the toughest experimental conditions that the most important discoveries are made.

Second, stockmarkets come as close as markets can get to being pure games. In other words, almost all the decisions made by the

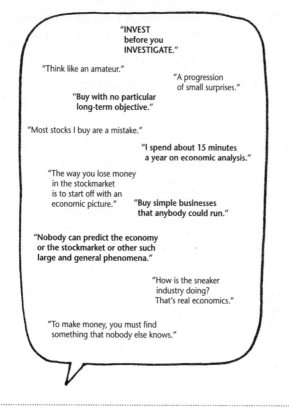

The contrarian wisdom of Peter Lynch

players are competitive in nature. For example, the day-to-day investment choices of fund managers are effectively moves in a game – and therefore quintessentially strategic. Also, the rules of the game, and what it means to win, are exceptionally simple. Winners are those who achieve the highest rates of return on the capital at their disposal.

Third, the strategic moves themselves can be simply described. They comprise the purchases and sales of financial instruments at discrete moments in time. These choices are also transparent. The information we need to specify the strategies of the competing fund managers are invariably in the public domain. This makes the study of stockmarkets far simpler and their interpretation more reliable than, for example, the study of manufacturing companies' strategies where it is notoriously difficult to know what particular strategy, if any, is being pursued.

Furthermore, the performance of an investment strategy is easy to measure. The value of a fund, for example, is continuously priced by the market in which it competes. This makes the relationship between strategy and performance much clearer and easier to analyse than in non-capital markets. This is helped by the fact that the impact of non-strategic factors on performance is minimal. Stockmarkets in Western economies are virtually level playing fields. Because of their efficiency, there are few unfair advantages available to any of the players. Effectively, the barriers to entry or exit are low. Scale advantages are minimal. Skills of implementation hardly play a part. The role of operations is incidental. Qualities of leadership, teamwork, interpersonal skills, emotional intelligence, trust – and all the other behavioural skills that can affect performance in a company – play a small part in the investment business. Luck has, at most, a short-term effect. There would seem to be no factors other than strategic skill to account for performance.

Looking for robust links between strategy and performance in the world of investing is made easier because many of the most successful investment managers have published their theories of investment and the assumptions underlying the strategies they have pursued.

Three celebrated fund managers, in particular, have become famous for their theories: Peter Lynch of the Magellan Fund, Warren Buffett of Berkshire Hathaway and George Soros of the Quantum Fund. What unites all three is that they each believed in constructing for themselves, as though from first principles, a set of operating criteria grounded in a personally invented model of market behaviour and successful investment. Their models were highly distinctive. But there were also some commonalities:

- **Contrarian** – they delighted in challenging investment orthodoxy, whether academic or professional.

- **Conjectural** – they were acutely aware of the fallibility of their own assumptions.

- **Transparent** – they sought to make their assumptions public and explicit, stating them in the form of testable propositions and inviting comment and criticism.

- **Inimitable** – however well-publicised their overall assumptions, behind them there was an irreducible element of tacit knowledge or "know-how" behind their models.

- **Experiential** – much of this know-how was garnered from acting in the market over a long period of time and not just from thinking about it.

- **Experimental** – its veracity depended upon continuous and purposeful experimentation.

- **Dynamic** – they recognised that the process of learning was never finished.

- **Adaptive** – they understood learning to mean continuously "hunting" or "tracking" the truth through a process of enlightened trial and error.

These principles, tempered over time in the furnace of highly competitive capital markets, betray a particular mindset. They cannot act as substitutes or shortcuts for the hard, first-hand thinking that the formulation of any particular corporate strategy demands, but they do suggest the frame of mind that is most likely to lead to effective strategic designs.

Most discoveries in business are the result of accident rather than design

Misconception: Monday to Friday between 9.00am and 6.00pm are the most fertile and productive hours of the working week

"Mould-breaking strategies grow initially like weeds; they are not cultivated like tomatoes in a hothouse." **Henry Mintzberg**

"A weed is a flower in the wrong place." **Ian Emberson**

"GET OUT OF YOUR OFFICE. Tell me, honestly, when was the last time that something inspiring, off-the-wall, counter-cultural or clever happened at that big table in your office?" Tom Peters, an exuberant writer on management, poses this arresting question as a prelude to reappraising the conditions that are particularly conductive to creativity, breakthrough thinking and strategic innovation. Peters has long held the view that luck is a critical contributor to corporate success, but, more contentiously, that luck can be "managed" to some extent:

> If you believe that success does owe a lot to luck, and that luck in turn owes a lot to getting in the way of unexpected opportunities, you need not throw up your hands in despair – there are strategies you can pursue to allow a little nuttiness into your life, and perhaps, get lucky.

What, then, are some of the ways of bumping into unexpected opportunities?

Peter Drucker believed that noticing the unexpected is the richest, least risky, most neglected source of innovation in business, far more so, for example, than the application of emerging scientific knowledge. Our expectations are the practical manifestation of our theories. So when the world takes us by surprise it is, in effect, challenging us to interrogate the belief that led to this false prediction. The more we attend to the unexpected and the more seriously we inquire into its source, the more we will spot opportunities for changing our beliefs and trying something new or different.

Placing ourselves purposefully in the way of unexpected opportunities can be seen as a way of deliberately crossing various kinds of boundaries. When we move into unfamiliar space we heighten not only our sensitivity to the unexpected but also the chance of encountering something new and thought-provoking.

Organisations, particularly companies, are replete with boundaries, all acting potentially as barriers to innovation: internal distinctions between departments, functions, levels and disciplines, as well as external distinctions between one business and another, whether supplier, customer or competitor. Moving only among those who share similar perspectives and qualifications sets a low ceiling on learning. It is when we escape into "foreign territory" that learning, imagination and innovation are revitalised. Advertising agencies that mix their core disciplines typically outperform those that keep them hermetically sealed in their own exclusive space. Typically, there are far more organisational restraints encouraging people to stay within their unit than there are mechanisms encouraging cross-boundary mixing. This is particularly true of the service and support functions in a business, such as finance, engineering, human resources and information technology.

Emphasising the importance of "peripheral vision", while lamenting its rarity, Peters once remarked that "the really interesting stuff is usually going on just beyond the margins of the professional's ever-narrowing line of sight".

There are four frontiers that, if crossed, stimulate the imagination: organisational, geographical, methodological and conceptual. Within a firm, the simple act of mixing people from different levels, functions and departments has the effect of generating richer conversations and opening up new perspectives. Management-development programmes are much more productive when, for example, participants escape the physical and intellectual confines of the lecture theatre and find themselves engaging in open conversation with people from walks of life very different from their own. Executives have far more to learn from artists, philosophers, athletes, composers, volunteers, journalists, soldiers and explorers than from other executives, however successful and however eminent. The enlightened trend in business schools towards "discovery programmes" and "learning journeys" recognises the power of these kinds of "accidental encounters".

The learning agendas of most companies are remarkably alike. For example, the brief that a company gives to a business school for the development of a training programme is much the same, whatever the company and whatever its industry. Topics will concentrate on leadership, strategic innovation and change management; and the tools will be a combination of lectures, case studies and 360-degree feedback. This covers probably 95% of the work that business schools do for their corporate clients. These paths are far too well trodden for any insights to emerge.

By contrast, the skill to ask different questions, to address a different agenda, or to pose different challenges is rare, but urgent. Even the smallest shift in the definition of a problem – or of an opportunity – can open up new options. Yet invariably companies are too busy seeking out solutions to pose unasked questions.

> Two roads diverged in a wood, and I …
> I took the one less travelled by,
> And that has made all the difference.
>
> **Robert Frost,** *The Road Not Taken*

⌬ Creative people give themselves more time to solve problems

Misconception: individual performance = personal
skill x long hours x hard work

"Most of us would do our jobs better if we did them less, not more."
Julie Burchill

"Thinking is more interesting than knowing, but less interesting than looking." **Goethe**

THINKING TAKES MANY FORMS. We can direct our attention either to the inner world of our thoughts and feelings, or to the external world of events and the happenings going on around us. And the gaze we bring to these two worlds can be either focused and specific or relaxed and diffuse.

The analytical style of thinking that we associate with philosophy is characterised by a focused attention upon the inner world. Philosophers value precision, clarity of reasoning and explicitness. The opposite, more contemplative style of thinking is associated more with the artist. Here the attention is softer and more inclusive, and is directed outwards to the external world. The artist, like the detective, is observing the whole effect but noticing the telling detail that injects meaning into the scene. The scientist, like the artist, directs his attention outwards but, unlike the artist, looks at the world through a particular lens, searching specifically for universal patterns. Scientific thinking is a form of scrutiny or purposeful inquiry. It knows what is significant before the act of looking, and is therefore able to screen out irrelevant detail. Lastly, there is thinking that is inward and diffuse. This is the world of

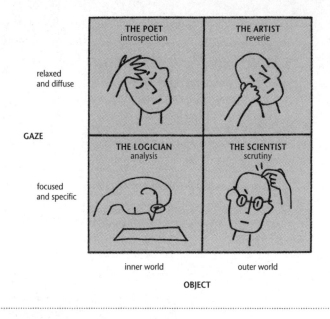

GAZE — relaxed and diffuse / focused and specific

| | THE POET — introspection | THE ARTIST — reverie |
| THE LOGICIAN — analysis | THE SCIENTIST — scrutiny |

inner world   outer world

OBJECT

Four ways of paying attention and having ideas

the poet. Introspection and soft focus characterise this style of thinking. The poet is comfortable with intuitive truths, subconscious thought and implicit ways of knowing.

In business, there is a strong bias towards explicit knowledge, cognitive thought and focused attention. Clarity of objectives, specificity of desired outcomes, transparency of reasoning, surfacing of assumptions, analysis of root causes and disciplined linearity of thought are taken to be the canons of professional management and organisational decision-making. For knowledge to count as a reliable basis for action, it has to be "packaged"; that is, codified in manuals, procedures, plans, presentations and expert systems. It is more important for a strategy to be logical than to possess insight or foresight. Reasoning is given greater weight than truth. What Jeffrey Pfeffer, a professor of organisational behaviour at Stanford University, has called "smart talk" – the bias towards articulacy – has come to dominate fuzzier, less structured, more intuitive approaches to the truth.

Artists and poets have a lot to teach strategists. They understand that creativity cannot be hurried. Sometimes we have to "wait on the truth". David McClelland, a psychologist, showed that what sets creative people apart from less creative people is the permission they give themselves to take longer to solve problems. They learn the habit of posting a question or a problem to the back of their mind, knowing that their subconscious mind will work on it without the need for deadlines. Then, without any warning, the solution will drop into consciousness. Less creative people in the meantime will have moved on, grappling quickly but ineffectively with the latest concern to have crossed their desk.

Generating knowledge will always be a scarcer skill and a more valuable activity than managing or codifying or disseminating or applying knowledge. But it is a rare organisation that acknowledges this fact. Business prefers to extol the virtues of decisiveness, pace and control, whereas the arts understand that the dream-like thinking that is sometimes called "musing" or "reverie" is the true wellspring of creativity.

⬿ An organisation's "bullshit quotient" is directly proportional to its disregard for the truth

• •

Misconception: bullshitting is less harmful than lying

• •

> "One of the most salient features of our culture is that there is so much bullshit." **Harry Frankfurt**

BULLSHIT HAS A LONG HISTORY. In ancient Greece it was called sophistry. Nowadays, it goes under the description of humbug, cant, imposture and quackery.

The bullshitter is not a liar – he does not set out deliberately to deceive – but neither does he take the truth very seriously. Indeed, it is his lack of concern for accuracy that makes him dangerous. The bullshitter does not presume to know the truth and therefore cannot be said to be lying. His offence is more worrying in a way, because he does not seem to be bothered one way or the other. He is indifferent to the distinction between truth and falsity. He regards the difference as immaterial and unimportant.

Harry Frankfurt, a moral philosopher at Princeton University, says:

> When we characterise talk as hot air, we mean that what comes out of the speaker's mouth is only that. It is mere vapour. His speech is empty, without substance or content. His use of language, accordingly, does not contribute to the purpose it purports to serve. No more information is communicated than if the speaker had merely exhaled. There are similarities between hot air and excrement, incidentally, which make hot air seem an especially suitable equivalent for bullshit.

A.

"The promise of reform which the Green Paper heralds holds much for the public and service alike; local policing, customised to local need with authentic answerability, strengthened accountabilities at force level through reforms to police authorities and HMIC, performance management at the service of localities with targets and plans tailored to local needs, the end of centrally engineered one size fits all initiatives, an intelligent approach to cutting red tape through redesign of processes and cultures, a renewed emphasis on strategic development so as to better equip our service to meet the amorphous challenges of managing cross force harms, risks and opportunities."

B.

"This government is committed to reform of public services to match the best in the world, and as a minister I am personally passionate about achieving this goal. My pledge to you is that I will put in place the building blocks. I will set the direction of travel. With my officials I will develop toolkits to undertake a robust interrogation of our working practices. I will address issues around the resourcing and management of change. My objective is nothing less than a dynamic, top-performing, cutting-edge service, fit for purpose for the 21st century. My target is an enhanced customer experience which will empower all our shareholders to access a wider and wider range of initiatives and opportunities. This government is about making choices. This government is about a vision for all the British people. It is a tremendous and exciting challenge, and one on which we will deliver!"

. . . .

The rising tide of sophistry: which is the spoof? A or B?

A is from a report by the Association of Chief Police Officers in response to a government Green Paper on policing.

B is by Peter Gasson in *The Spectator* (October 14th 2006) – it was his winning entry for a competition to provide a specimen of ministerial waffle.

Just as hot air is speech that has been emptied of all informative content, so excrement is matter from which everything nutritive has been removed.

Bullshit is offensive and destructive not just because it misrepresents the world it seems to be describing or indeed the views of the person who is speaking, but more importantly because it misrepresents the speaker's intentions and motives. Liars know the difference between what is true and what is false, take the distinction seriously, and purposefully seek to subvert the truth and deceive others. Conversely, bullshitters have little interest in whether their utterances are true or false.

Bullshit is to be expected whenever someone feels impelled by the situation to say something profound but lacks entirely the knowledge to do so. The occasion overwhelms the individual and, in place of sense, highfalutin nonsense is uttered. There seems to be no way out. Either you speak, taking the risk that your cover will be blown, or you remain silent and lose face. Bullshit is face-saving on a brazen scale.

The bullshit quotient is high in today's business world because more and more people are called upon publicly to make sense of a world that is increasingly complex and unpredictable. The words "I don't know" seem to have become an inadmissible response.

⌘ Strategy is more dependent on courage and humility than talent and charisma

Misconception: leaders need to be charismatic

"We dream vaguely; but we dread precisely." **Anon**

IF YOU ASK CEOS TO NOMINATE the business leaders they have most admired, they will invariably refer to a small group of well-known, highly entrepreneurial men at the top of large corporations: leaders such as Richard Branson, Warren Buffett, Bill Gates, Steve Jobs and Alan Lafley. If you then ask them to say what precisely they admire about these great figures, they will point to their bravery, their decisiveness, the boldness of their vision, their contrarian beliefs, the originality of their strategies, the courage of their convictions, their self-confidence and willpower. But if you now inquire into what strategies and policies they themselves are advocating in their own businesses, the answers that you get are depressingly familiar: cost reduction, 360-degree feedback, outsourcing, downsizing, margin improvement, shared services, process re-engineering and change programmes.

Richard Rumelt, who invented this research ruse, makes the observation that the actions of most executives fall far short of their aspirations and ideals. He wonders why. How can such a yawning gap between the reality and the rhetoric of business be explained?

Rumelt defines strategy as "the predatory leap" that transforms the competitive landscape and which is such a feature of the leaders that their peers admire. He describes the pedestrian policies that most business leaders actually adopt as "doorknob polishing". Why, in positions of great power, do so many CEOs settle for polishing doorknobs?

When CEOs are asked at the end of their career, "What do you wish you'd done differently?", they nearly all say something along these lines: "I wish I'd acted with greater speed and courage" – though admittedly they now have the hindsight to reduce the uncertainties they felt at the time. So what is it about the context of business that inhibits CEOs from doing what they know needs doing? Why do they prevaricate? What is holding them back? Why the failure of nerve?

In keeping with our belief that performance is determined more by the system than by the individual, perhaps the CEO is placed in an impossible position. The notion of "charismatic leadership" is a hellish burden to bear. Jeffrey Pfeffer has demonstrated that CEOs are encouraged to believe that they are "in control of their companies". Politicians are placed in much the same bind. As a result leaders find themselves stuck between a rock and hard place – that is, between their egotistical need to succeed and the overblown expectations that organisations place on them. The fear of failure erodes their self-confidence and standardises their thinking. The victim of society's faith in leadership ends up being the leader himself. Followers could be forgiven for feeling some degree of *Schadenfreude* in the fall from grace of those they put on too high a pedestal.

⬤ Competition compensates for its own wastefulness by the pace of innovation that it spawns

Misconception: capitalism is only as admirable as the motives of capitalists

"If the past century of economic policymaking has taught us anything, it is that achieving strong long-term growth often has less to do with macroeconomic policies than with good microeconomics, including fostering competitive markets that reward innovation and restricting government to only a limited role." **The Economist**

SINCE 1820, THE WORLD POPULATION has grown sixfold, world GDP almost 50-fold, and world GDP per head roughly tenfold. But averages hide huge variations in performance. For example, GDP per head has increased almost 30-fold in Japan and 20-fold in western Europe, America and Australasia, compared with fivefold growth in the rest of the world. Why is there this massive difference? Why have some parts of the world grown four times as fast as others? The unambiguous answer is that they are the beneficiaries of dynamic market economies.

Markets dramatically outperform command economies because they are better at solving five problems crucial to wealth creation:

- enabling buyers, through the free flow of reliable information, to have confidence in what they are buying;
- enabling buyers and sellers, though such mechanisms as legally binding contracts, to trust each others' promises;

- fostering and policing fair and open competition between suppliers;
- instituting and protecting property rights;
- mitigating the collateral damage that markets can cause to third parties.

By developing increasingly ingenious solutions to these problems, the market has evolved, particularly over the last 200 years, into what Martin Wolf has called "a complex and sophisticated piece of institutional machinery" based on the foundational principles of freedom of contract, the right to property and the rule of law (framed and enforced by the state).

Vaclav Havel, a writer and the first president of the Czech Republic, said:

> Though my heart may be left of centre, I have always known that the only economic system that works is a market economy. This is the only natural economy, the only kind that makes sense, the only one that leads to prosperity, because it is the only one that reflects the nature of life itself. The essence of life is infinitely and mysteriously multiform, and therefore it cannot be contained or planned for, in its fullness and variability, by any central intelligence.

Markets are particularly good at stimulating human creativity. For 200 years the world has witnessed an extraordinary growth in economic prosperity. It has become clear that wherever political and economic conditions favour a dynamic market economy, the result is always dramatic material progress, among the poor as well as the rich. Writing about the role of business in the modern world, David Henderson, an economist, has observed that:

> The principal direct impulse to economic progress in recent decades has come from profit-related activities and initiatives on the part of business enterprises working within the framework of a competitive market economy. This business contribution results from the twin stimuli that a market economy provides: wide-ranging entrepreneurial opportunities and pervasive competitive pressures. The two aspects are inseparable, since the competitive pressures

> arise from market opportunities that are themselves opened up by economic freedom.
>
> From an economy-wide perspective, now as in the past, the primary role of business is to act as a vehicle for economic progress. The role is not, and cannot be, "internalised" by enterprises themselves. Economic progress does not depend on a commitment by businesses to bring it about.

Henderson is adamant that the benefits of capitalism do not depend upon individual beneficence. The results flow from the process of competition itself and not from the motives of the competitors. Individualism operating in a market economy will have a much larger impact on social well-being than collectivism operating in a planned economy.

Self-interest, upon which markets depend for their efficiency, is not the same as selfishness. Individuals exercising self-interest in a market economy will generally enrich each other as actors in a positive-sum game, whereas selfishness is behaviour at the expense of another. There is nothing in the free exchange of goods for money that requires the notion of selfishness to explain it.

Innovation is the driving force of capitalism. In his book *The Free-Market Innovation Machine*, William Baumol, an economist, shows that innovation, not price competition (the preferred explanation of classical economists), is the engine of the market process. Companies that do not bring new solutions to the market risk falling behind their competitors and ultimately going out of business. Most of the innovations that create economic value originate within existing companies. Indeed, innovation is an utterly routine activity of the modern business enterprise. On average, innovation is not particularly profitable. In the main, it is "a numbers game", where some get lucky but many lose out. The incentive to keep innovating is less the lure of profit and more the fear of failure. Thus the market is wired up to encourage the entrepreneurial spirit in organisations both large and small.

PART 3

Organisation and management

"The more corporate executives believe in a free (unregulated) market, the more they believe in a regulated internal market." **Russell Ackoff**

TODAY'S BUSINESS CLIMATE is generally seen as uniquely challenging. Many executives describe market conditions as difficult, stressful and ambiguous. They admit to feeling confused, frustrated and pressured. They wonder whether business conditions will ever "return to normal". They fear that turbulence, uncertainty and discontinuity have become permanent features of the managerial landscape.

These are the two most popular clichés:

- The only constant is change.
- The pace of change is accelerating.

Other platitudes are that customers are more discerning, shareholders are more impatient, competitors are more aggressive and employees are more demanding. (The mirror image of these assumptions is that, once upon a time, there was a golden age of plentiful demand, pliant customers, passive competitors, supine staff and easy profits.) It is rare for today's widely held beliefs to be questioned, let alone tested. They are simply accepted as central truths of the modern condition.

Executives typically explain these pressures as originating in the external world. They see the drivers of change as advances in technology, shifts of demography, trends in lifestyle, changes of regulatory regime and the globalisation of business. Interestingly, they see these forces as originating outside the firm and operating mercilessly on the firm. They are unlikely to claim that they themselves are responsible for accelerating change.

How do executives cope with a world that they perceive as turbulent, unpredictable and threatening? One response is to make a determined attempt to isolate the firm from these external forces by taking tighter control of the internal corporate environment. This usually means adopting a more disciplined management style: a focus on the essentials, greater attention to costs, a resolve to squeeze out waste, strict adherence to the principles of lean thinking and total quality management (TQM), adoption of the language of conformance, a certain scepticism towards intrapreneurial initiatives – such as experimentation or investment in new and untried business models – and, overall, a preference for optimising the current operating model rather than inventing radically new ones. The results of all this belt-tightening, however, are not always rewarding. All too often, revenues will have shrunk faster than costs.

As observers of the business scene over the past 20 years, we have noticed a default to three basic forms of behaviour when the pressures on performance become acute:

● Decision-making is centralised. Firms only make decisions that can be strongly corroborated by incontrovertible evidence; speculative or experimental investments are shunned.

● Greater alignment is sought. Firms pursue transformational development programmes for their people, designed either to bring individual behaviour into line with the company's espoused values or to raise individual skills to the level of some desired "competency profile".

- Personal accountability is emphasised. Reliance is placed upon a plethora of targets, metrics and incentives to "drive" performance and hold managers responsible for "meeting their commitments".

We believe that these stereotypical responses to pressure serve only to increase the pressure; that the pressures themselves are largely self-induced rather than emanating from the external world; that as a result of this combination of perceived threat, aversion to risk, pessimism and safety-first management, corporate performance deteriorates still further; and that a completely different set of economic and psychological assumptions is needed if firms are not to fall foul of this self-destructive pattern of behaviour.

We need a radically different model of managerial behaviour and organisational effectiveness.

🌑 The horns of the managerial dilemma are the need to be in control and the need to be continuously learning

"Everyone doing their best is not the answer. Everyone is doing their best." **W. Edwards Deming**

"Management by numerical goal is an attempt to manage without knowledge of what to do." **W. Edwards Deming**

RUNNING A SUCCESSFUL BUSINESS IS DIFFICULT. Part of the difficulty lies in performing two contrasting tasks simultaneously. The first task is administration; the second is innovation. Skilful administration extols the virtues of clarity, order and predictability; it deals in the currency of targets, measures and incentives; its values are those of direction, efficiency and control; its goal is the perfectly aligned, tightly integrated and logically coherent organisation. By contrast, skilful innovation celebrates the virtues of creativity, playfulness and growth; it is at ease with a measure of confusion, ambiguity and disorder – indeed, it often flourishes best at "the edge of chaos"; it trades in the currency of hypotheses, experiments and insights; its values are those of courage, independence of thought, open dialogue and truth; its nirvana is a state of "flow" where ideas and discoveries are natural and profuse.

However, a perfectly aligned business that takes no risks, tries nothing new and never makes discoveries is destined ultimately to fail; likewise, a business that is dedicated only to discovery, pays no heed to organisation, dispenses with anything resembling a structure, a system or a process, and ignores its cost base is not sustainable. The art is to build both capabilities into the

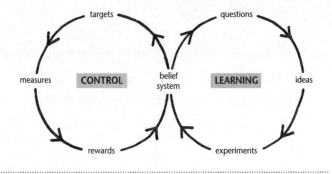

Performance management: balancing the virtues of control and learning

organisation and to maintain a balance between the two. The tension is between conformity and adventure; control and exploration; defence and advance; alignment and discovery.

Alignment is the process of ensuring that a company's goals (such as the key performance indicators structured to be appropriate to all levels of the organisation), metrics (such as the scorecard against which the delivery of these performance targets is continuously calibrated) and rewards (such as the system of incentives for recognising and remunerating those who deliver on their targets) are mutually reinforcing and supportive of the strategic intent of the business. It is the pursuit of efficiency through control.

By contrast, discovery embraces the spirit of restless questioning (such as interrogating one's own assumptions), the process of forming options and ideas (especially tentative answers to these questions) and the design of experiments (with the aim of testing the viability of these ideas). When things are not working well, the mentality of discovery is to ask deeper, more searching questions, to generate braver, more imaginative options and to design tougher, more discriminating tests, thereby opening up new possibilities. It is the pursuit of effectiveness through learning.

It has been said that today's corporations are 19th-century

	CONTROL: one horn of the managerial dilemma	LEARNING: the other horn of the managerial dilemma
model of performance management	alignment of strategic intent, targets, metrics and rewards	culture of questioning, speculating, experimenting and transforming
logic of organisational progress (Chris Argyris)	single-loop learning: bringing performance into line with budget expectations	double-loop learning: testing the assumptions driving the budget expectations
overarching managerial task	efficiency: doing things right	effectiveness: doing the right thing
assumed sources of corporate success	focus, discipline and humility (Jim Collins)	creativity, courage and a cause worth serving (Gary Hamel)
definition of rationality in business	exploiting knowledge: the application of scientific discoveries	making discoveries: the application of the scientific method
the role of facts in inquiry	to provide the raw material for getting new ideas	to provide the ammunition for discarding obsolete ideas
the role of plans and planning	promises: to make commitments by which to be judged	propositions: to surface assumptions about which to learn
quality management (Tom Peters)	minimising things going wrong	maximising things going right
critical success factors (Sumantra Ghoshal)	control, constraint, contract and compliance	stretch, trust, self-discipline and support
dominant managerial orientation (Wolfgang Grulke)	looking inwards to process, structure and system for the next idea	looking outwards to users, markets and discoveries for the next idea
greatest source of threat (Corporate Strategy Board)	external factors	internal factors
the most dangerous competitor	our largest or fastest growing or least noticed competitor	our own complacency or myopia or paranoia
the art of new product development	improving the hit rate (the probability of success per trial)	increasing the number of hits (the number of trials per time period)
behaviour towards mistake-makers	upbraiding those who tried new things that went wrong	upbraiding those who didn't try new things that, if tried, could have gone right
the dark side	making happen what will happen anyway	anarchic pursuit of anything and everything that comes up

Balancing the virtues of control and learning: varying interpretations

institutions pursuing 20th-century strategies to be executed by 21st-century talent. This book argues that the modern corporation has struck the wrong balance between alignment and discovery. The emergence of what has been called "Management 2.0", echoing the notion of Web 2.0, is a belated move to redress the balance away from unremitting command and control and towards greater curiosity and experimentation.

The primary role of management is to motivate employees and co-ordinate their activities

"The large corporation that emerged in the late 19th and early 20th centuries was built on a military model of organisation: everyone had their place in a rank, every place defined a function, and authority flowed through the chain of command from top to bottom." **Charles Leadbeater**

THE ORIGINAL PURPOSE OF MANAGEMENT, and the role it was given, was to take unskilled men off the land and to integrate them into co-ordinated working units to perform complex tasks in the pioneering manufacturing plants that were being built at the close of the 19th century. Authority and bureaucracy were management's most powerful tools. Max Weber, one of the first great theorists of capitalism, wrote glowingly of the civilising and egalitarian power of bureaucracy. The emphasis was on contract, control, compliance and co-ordination – putting people to work on tasks that collectively met organisational goals efficiently.

The world has moved on, both socially and technically, since 1890, but the core principles of management have hardly changed. What has changed is that people today are less inclined to go to work to comply or to be controlled or to act as the agents of others, whether bosses or shareholders. They want to serve their own interests, albeit in an organisational setting with commercial goals. They go to work to express their talent, to mix their skills with others to create a common product or service of which they can be proud. The job of management today is less to reinforce

hierarchical ⟵————————⟶ **democratic**

Do managers get their power from the office they hold or from the people who choose to be led by them?

strategic ⟵————————⟶ **opportunistic**

Are decisions made in line with a pre-ordained plan or in response to an unpredictable and unfolding reality?

individual ⟵————————⟶ **collective**

Is knowledge found in the distributed expertise of specialists or in the synthesised wisdom of the crowd?

bureaucratic ⟵————————⟶ **adhocratic**

Is know-how codified in standard operating procedures or applied as the changing situation demands?

extrinsic ⟵————————⟶ **intrinsic**

Are employees motivated by carrots and sticks or by the joys and sorrows of the work itself?

instrumental ⟵————————⟶ **ethical**

Are employees treated as means to an end ("human resources") or as ends in themselves ("resourceful humans")?

Six dimensions on which any model of management is positioned

the organisational structure than to mitigate its toxic effects and liberate the imaginative powers of those working within it.

Management is a social technology for bringing people together to achieve extraordinary results. Whatever the management model, there are six tasks that must be performed if the organisation is to prosper:

- **Coherence** – the need to provide direction, focus, legitimacy and forward momentum for the organisation.
- **Catalysis** – the need to stimulate the energy and enthusiasm

that people bring to their work and to the workplace.

- **Commitment** – the need to create a widespread sense of personal responsibility for the success of the enterprise.
- **Capability** – the need to develop methods of working that promote business effectiveness and efficiency.
- **Co-ordination** – the need to ensure that every element of the organisation is more effective for being part of the whole.
- **Control** – the need to create a governance structure that monitors the performance of the main elements of the business.

What is in contention is not the purpose of management, as defined in these six core tasks, but the methods by which practising managers try to fulfil them. Many of the assumptions that managers bring to the task are antiquated. For example, the job of management is not to manage people to fit the organisation but to manage (and design) the organisation to draw upon – and draw out – the skills and aspirations of the human beings who live within it.

〰 Six operating principles underpin the managerial model of most organisations

··

THE SITUATION THAT CREATED THE NEED for management in its original 19th-century form no longer exists. Since the invention of this method of co-ordination and motivation, the world of work has changed beyond recognition – but the model of management remains roughly what it was 130 years ago. As a result, the "standard model of management", and the ethos surrounding it, has become the performance bottleneck in most companies.

The belief system on which it is based comprises six maxims that can best be described as "half truths". These maxims can be defined as follows:

- **Hierarchy of power** – the belief that order, cohesion and decisiveness require a strong degree of autocracy; that power is best concentrated in few hands; that the knowledge and good judgment required to exercise such power are possessed by few people; that people with these talents are easily recognised; that most people are happy to surrender some of their autonomy to this minority; and that the alternatives to this model are impractical or too dire to contemplate.

- **Singularity of purpose** – the belief that, just as every pyramid has a single summit, so every organisation needs a single goal; that the perfect alignment of everyone around a shared set of aims, values, beliefs and policies is the necessary condition for organisational success; that experimentation should be limited to means and not ends; and that most people are motivated by the discipline of adhering to a centrally established set of norms.

- **Specialisation of task** – the belief that division of labour leads to efficiency; that most people can master only a small part of any complex, collective task; that mastery comes only with practice and therefore multi-tasking carries risks to organisational performance; that the ideal work package is scaled to the capability and capacity of individuals, not teams; that therefore the job rather than the project is the best building block of an organisation; and that most people give more of their best when held personally accountable for a job well done than when held jointly responsible for a project successfully achieved.

- **Standardisation of process** – the belief that there is a right way to do things; that one size does indeed fit all; that standard operating procedures efficiently co-ordinate the activities of many people; that a good process, like an expert system, encodes the wisdom of experience; that, as experience grows, processes are easily and continuously modified to take account of this new knowledge; and that most people are content to comply with a well-designed, clearly formulated method of working.

- **Planning of outcomes** – the belief that the single most important management process is that of strategic planning since it underpins all others; that co-ordination is impossible without the "visible hand" of a carefully choreographed, top-down, annually programmed set of forecasts, targets and outcomes; that, in its essentials, the future is predictable enough for senior executives to formulate reliable and robust plans; and that most people are willing to place their trust in budgeting as a fair, transparent and motivating process conducted by all parties in good faith and with a minimum of "politics".

- **Motivation by money** – the belief that people can be paid to perform; that money is the great motivator (followed closely by status, itself best symbolised by wealth); that people respond to financial incentives in an obvious and predictable manner; that they do not feel manipulated or diminished by it; that they are not tempted to game the system; and that, offered a trade-off between income and job satisfaction, they will be inclined to take the money.

These six sets of assumptions are becoming threadbare. Overly strict adherence to them has now become a source of serious economic inefficiency and human malaise.

⚘ The dark side of the standard model of management is increasingly constraining performance

....

"The barren delusion called 'managerialism' may soon be defunct. It has reached its dead end." **Matthew Parris**

EACH OF THE SIX OPERATING PRINCIPLES manifests itself in a range of beliefs and everyday work practices that are becoming increasingly dysfunctional:

- **Hierarchy of power** relies upon the deference of subordinates to bosses for it to work. This can result in a culture of passivity and learned helplessness laced with fear and timidity. Organisations come to bear an uncomfortable resemblance to class-based societies. Distinctions between management and worker, between white collar and blue collar, between office and shop floor, between salaried and hourly paid are essentially caste distinctions. Original thought remains the province of a senior cadre of executives.

- **Singularity of purpose** finds echoes in similar phrases such as "common objectives", "strategic intent", "unity of vision" and "shared values". The implicit assumption is that alignment, consensus and unanimity are all unqualified blessings in the context of a purposeful organisation. Diversity of viewpoint and plurality of values are deemed to be unhelpful. The unhealthy side-effects of unanimity are that it crowds out curiosity, inhibits debate, fosters "group think" and reinforces myopia. In effect, it bets the farm on a

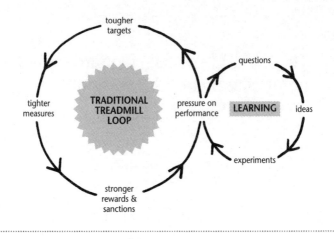

The default to the control loop when times get tough

single viewpoint. When there is only one authorised version of the future, and every other viewpoint is blasphemous, the structure has become perilously brittle.

● **Specialisation of task** assumes that the organisation can be chunked up cleanly into mutually exclusive and exhaustive jobs, each allocated to an individual "holder". Thus the job becomes the ultimate silo. It may look neat on an organisation chart but it hinders co-operation, hampers dialogue and limits learning; and by emphasising personal accountability and making it easier to point the finger of blame when things go wrong, it penalises entrepreneurship and engenders a risk-averse mindset.

● **Standardisation of method** is closely related to the quest for best practice. For example, the fashion for business process re-engineering has been driven essentially by the fear of being left behind. The assumption that the solution is obvious and that therefore skills of implementation are what distinguish winners from losers breeds a culture of compliance. Most change programmes are top-down

Best practice – the recipe for formulaic sameness	
Operational excellence – doorknob polishing	
Competitive benchmarking – plagiarism run riot	
Balanced scorecards – the bureaucrat's revenge	
Performance targets – insults for the conscientious	
Annual budgets – the pathology of under-ambition	
Financial incentives – bribes for loners and cynics	
Organisational alignment – the fear of diversity	
Shared values – the extinction of individualism	
Professional standards – box-ticking for the risk-averse	
Charismatic leadership – narcissism unbound	

Eleven telltale symptoms of a management model biased in favour of control at the expense of learning

initiatives that get their self-righteousness from the unfounded belief that "people resist change". Faith in panaceas stifles creativity and kills variety.

● **Planning of outcomes** rests on the assumption that the future can be written with the same confidence and accuracy as the past. Because planning is, by its nature, a top-down process, it has to assume a high degree of clairvoyance among the senior executives who are the authors, or at least the assessors, of these plans. Most plans are blueprints. When the day-to-day work of most employees is absorbed simply in the task of deploying plans, keeping promises, hitting targets, scoring quick wins and making the numbers, anything remotely opportunistic is drowned in a sea of fatalism. Planning infantilises employees.

● **Motivation by money**, which lies at the heart of what is sometimes called a bonus culture, assumes that nothing exceptional gets done by people in the absence of a financial incentive to do so. Alfie Kohn, who writes about human behaviour and social theory, calls this the bribery model of management. The downside of a bonus culture is that no one puts themselves out unless a reward is offered. What used to be called "pride in a job well done", a form of intrinsic motivation, is treated (erroneously) as a sentiment from another age. The problem with this method of motivation is that it demeans people, breeds cynicism, provides an excuse for greed and crowds out the spirit of voluntarism that is the inspiration of so much good work done in the world.

The dark side of management has become even darker since the credit crunch of 2008, with many stressed organisations defaulting to these antiquated and biased assumptions.

⬲ Six global forces are reducing the need for management

....

> "Battered by new sources of competition and new demands from customers, bombarded by investors, bemused and undermined by technology, buffeted by ideologies like empowerment that challenge the assumptions of hierarchy and control and beleaguered by recent academic attacks on head offices and other central overheads, the structure and behaviour of large corporations appear to be anachronistic and overdue for change." **Richard Koch and Ian Godden**

JUST AS FEUDAL SOCIETIES ultimately fell into disrepair and disrepute because they failed to keep pace with changing human aspirations and values, so the managerial model of organisational life is in danger of becoming just as obsolete. Six particular forces are alive today that are challenging both the legitimacy of managerial power and the wisdom of managerial elites:

- **Customer-centricity.** Making the customer the focus of every activity within the firm has the effect of dramatically reducing the need for administrative overheads. Judged against the criterion of customer value, most managerial activity is wasteful and self-indulgent. As the firm is turned through 90 degrees, from "vertically" serving the boss to "horizontally" serving the customer, large swathes of activity lose their validity. In particular, managers who are simply managing other managers are "found out".

- **Information technology.** As customers, shareholders and operatives become increasingly well-informed, the management structures connecting them become decreasingly necessary. Most managers, particularly middle managers, owe their jobs to having privileged access to data. Because well-designed, distributed IT systems remove this privilege, they have been able to reduce dramatically the number of management jobs, effectively disintermediating most managerial work. IT empowers "doers", owners and customers at the expense of managers.

- **Shareholder pressures.** With the stronger assertion of investor power and the trend towards shareholder metrics, various devices have been used to align managers ("the agents") with the interests of the owners ("the principals"). As the pressures to perform mount, and as the performance of managers becomes increasingly transparent, fewer and fewer managers are found to add economic value.

- **Global competition.** The power of investors and customers to exert cost and quality pressures on companies is hugely strengthened by free trade, deregulation and global competition. National economies, domestic-market leaders and geographical cartels can no longer escape the leanest or most reputable producer, wherever they happen to be located in the world. As Richard Koch, an entrepreneur and writer, puts it, "The ideology of capitalism has shifted from cost-plus to price-minus." Management is invariably the sacrificial victim.

- **Economies of simplicity.** Growth has long been the touchstone of most corporate strategies, the assumption being that scale creates greater cost economies and a more defendable advantage than any other factor. But with scale comes complexity in the form of proliferating products, fragmenting markets, matrix organisations, burgeoning transaction costs and a superstructure of co-ordinators, planners and head-office executives. The truth is dawning that economies of simplicity are a surer recipe for success than scale and scope, mainly because fewer managers are needed.

- **Faith in leaders.** In the 21st century, MBA graduates aspire to become change agents, or coaches, or leaders rather than managers. Unlike managers, leaders do not need a structure through which to transmit challenges, messages and instructions, or receive information, ideas and feedback. Leaders operate differently: they rely upon their personal chemistry; they work on people's sense of purpose, sense of identity and sense of belonging; they put their trust in people rather than systems to maintain control. They see layer upon layer of management as an obstacle, not an enabler.

At the top of many corporate agendas today should be the imperative of finding ways of un-managing, de-managing and counter-managing the organisation.

⟐ The internet is disintermediating management

....

MARSHALL MCLUHAN'S PRONOUNCEMENT 50 years ago that "the medium is the message" was remarkably prescient, given the invention since then of the world wide web and its associated social-media technologies. Natural conversations among people who have never met – and barely know each other – are dismantling totalitarian regimes, solving scientific problems, auctioning second-hand goods, constructing works of art, designing software solutions and writing encyclopedias without any form of managerial intervention or mediation.

The world has never been so connected, nor have conversations across so many boundaries been so easy or so productive. Self-organising communities of interest are springing up everywhere to create new forms of economic value.

When Jack Welch, a former CEO of General Electric, talked about the "boundariless organisation" as a utopian ideal, he could not have known that within ten years the technology required to realise this vision would be in worldwide use.

The glue that creates these communities no longer has to be an employment bond or an institutional affiliation or an organisational loyalty. All that is necessary is a common purpose and a spontaneous desire to collaborate, however loosely or intermittently. Groups united simply by a common interest or a shared problem or a complementary skill can find each other easily on the net and initiate a project or a campaign. The ease and simplicity of communication, not just the extraordinary access to information, has the potential to revolutionise the way work is done.

The collective wisdom that can be unlocked by Web 2.0 and 3.0 tools is encouraging and enabling the radical transformation of management models in existing organisations. A new set of management principles is coming to the fore that:

- draw upon larger, more diverse pools of talented people than those who happen to work full-time for the corporation;
- enable customers, user groups and other interested stakeholders to co-create the products and services of the future;
- relinquish control of methods and work practices to those employees who would prefer to escape the traditional work routines and operate instead in self-organising work groups of their own choosing.

The quality of conversation has been changed in certain respects by the new social media. The net allows far more people to be engaged in the same conversation; it encourages a greater diversity of opinion to be expressed; and it facilitates a more natural, playful and eclectic style of interaction, if only because the participants are anonymous. Power, position and title count for less. Conversations are unadjudicated and among equals. Every voice has equal weight. It is the content of the idea, not its source, that counts. Ideas stand or fall on their own merit.

⚫ The double bind is the defining condition of organisational man

"They are playing a game. They are playing at not playing a game. If I show them I see they are, I shall break the rules and they will punish me. I must play their game, of not seeing I see the game." **R.D. Laing**

MANAGED ORGANISATIONS create the conditions under which effective communication – and therefore interpersonal trust – is made particularly difficult. It presents its "victims" with a variety of dilemmas that are seemingly irreconcilable. Gregory Bateson, an anthropologist and social scientist, has given the name "double bind" to just such dilemmas. A double bind is "a situation in which no matter what a person does, he can't win". It was originally put forward as an explanation of schizophrenia by Bateson, Donald Jackson, Jay Haley and John Weakland in 1956, but it is increasingly seen as offering valuable insights into the complexities of everyday communication. A double bind is the dilemma experienced by an individual receiving two conflicting demands to which there can be no satisfactory logical response and about which no discussion or inquiry is allowed.

Human communication is fraught with difficulty, partly because much of what is communicated is either implied or contextual, and non-verbal cues are often critical. In a power structure where the consequences of confusion, misinterpretation or disobedience are serious, the difficulties are accentuated. For example, a demand is made by a boss of a subordinate but the demand itself is inherently impossible to fulfil because some contextual factor forbids it. This is how Bateson defined the double bind:

The logic of the double bind as captured in one of R.D. Laing's "Knots"

- The situation involves at least two individuals (or groups), one of which can be characterised as the "victim". The other is a figure of authority that the victim respects.

- The double bind is experienced by the victim, not as a single troubling episode, but as a recurring pattern of distressing experiences.

- A "primary injunction" is imposed upon the victim by his nemesis in one of two forms – "Do X or I will punish you" or "Do not do X or I will punish you".

- The punishment could be the withdrawal of trust or respect, the expression of anger or disapproval, or the display of helplessness or hopelessness.

- A "secondary injunction" is imposed that conflicts with the first at a higher level of abstraction, such as "Do what I said, but only do it because you genuinely want to do so". This injunction may be implied rather than spoken.

- A "tertiary injunction" is imposed – often tacitly – that prevents the victim from evading the dilemma.

The essence of a double bind is two irreconcilable demands, each on a different logical plane, neither of which can be ignored or avoided, which leave the victim caught on the horns of a dilemma, so that whichever demand they seek to satisfy, the other cannot be met. The victim's response to such a dilemma is something like: "I must do it, but I can't do it."

A Zen Buddhist master uses the device of the *koan* to place the student in a double bind that acts as a therapeutic tool of enlightenment. For example, the master asks the student, "Show me who you really are". There is nothing that the student can do, and also nothing he cannot do, to be authentic and to present his true self. In this way, the student learns the Buddhist concept of *anatman* (non-self).

In business, employees are presented every day with a stream of double-bind injunctions – each of them a kind of corporate *koan*:

- You must respect me.
- Set your own goals.
- If this were your own business, what would you do?
- Act as a leader: be yourself – with skill.
- Be spontaneous.
- How are we doing?
- Feel free to be candid and say exactly what is on your mind.
- It's not my job to tell you what to do, but what I suggest is that …
- Are you with us – or against us?
- Challenge orthodoxy! Break the rules! Bet the farm!
- Put all your effort into simply being yourself.
- Give me your honest feedback.
- Think the unthinkable.
- Just do it!

≋ Paranoia is the dominant mood of management

> "The most fundamental assumption of the underground managerial world is that truth is a good idea when it is not embarrassing or threatening – the very conditions under which truth is especially needed." **Chris Argyris**

MANAGERS ARE PLACED in an invidious position. They are expected to compete with their peers for promotion to the next level, while also being exemplary team players, collaborating naturally and generously with their colleagues. They are expected to be entrepreneurs, putting their career and financial security at risk on behalf of the shareholder, while also serving as model bureaucrats and corporate citizens, complying dutifully and selflessly with every regulation and rule placed in their way. They are expected to be the agents of the shareholders, aligning their own interests with those of the owners, while also acting with integrity as leaders, being true to their own values and exercising their own judgment. They are expected to create shareholder value, while also being encouraged to balance the interests of a wide variety of other stakeholders whose claims on the firm may be weaker and less obvious but whose ability to stir up trouble is all too evident.

The job of the modern manager is indeed imbued with ambiguity, internal contradictions and stressful demands. Little wonder that most managers respond to these pressures with a degree of perfectly rational, Machiavellian cunning. Putting their own self-interest and survival at the heart of their concerns, they typically play a clever game of appearing to grapple "authentically" with

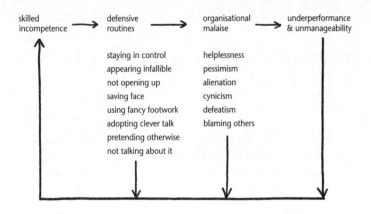

skilled incompetence	defensive routines	organisational malaise	underperformance & unmanageability
	staying in control	helplessness	
	appearing infallible	pessimism	
	not opening up	alienation	
	saving face	cynicism	
	using fancy footwork	defeatism	
	adopting clever talk	blaming others	
	pretending otherwise		
	not talking about it		

Self-reinforcing cycles of "skilled incompetence" and "learned helplessness"

Source: Adapted from Chris Argyris, *Overcoming Organizational Defenses: Facilitating Organizational Learning*, Prentice Hall, 1990

these challenges while being careful to do nothing that might endanger their career or blot their copybook.

The pattern is one where executives say bold, insightful and clever things while enacting rather dull, conventional and banal policies. Modern managers talk a good game. But their deeds rarely measure up to their rhetoric. And they have every reason to behave in this way. Any rational person with a healthy instinct for self-preservation would adopt these habits. Managers know full well that words count for more than deeds in the modern organisation (mesmerised as it is by the fashion for visionary goals, stretch targets, strategic plans, codes of conduct, rules of engagement and statements of values). They know that, in the reputation stakes, mistakes carry more weight than triumphs. They know that, faced with risk and the possibility of error, discretion is the better part of valour. And they know that meeting internal targets and performing well against key performance indicators will always deliver more kudos than the creation of competitive advantage for the enterprise as a whole.

In short, the "self-protective virtues" of staying in control, reining in your emotions, giving little away, being circumspect, not providing hostages to fortune, not upsetting people, saving face and protecting others' face are the essential skills of organisational survival. The principle that most accurately captures the spirit of the managerial workplace is the saying: "We dream vaguely, but we dread precisely." Dread is a stronger driver of executive behaviour than dreaming. But, of course, if everyone adopted these tactics then nothing much would be achieved and the firm would suffer. The challenge is to create an organisational context that makes it safe for people to exercise critical thinking, rather in the manner of scientists in a lab.

The need for extraordinary management suggests a poorly designed organisation

"Workers work within a system that – try as they might – is beyond their control. It is the system, not their individual skills, that determines how they perform." **W. Edwards Deming**

THERE IS NO EVIDENCE that the best companies employ the best people, or that the more talented the employees, the more successful the firm. Jeffrey Pfeffer has observed that ordinary people working in extraordinary organisations typically outperform extraordinary people working in ordinary organisations; and W. Edwards Deming, a statistician best known for his work in Japan on high-quality manufacturing, argued convincingly that organisational context counts for 90% of performance. Yet context remains relatively unmanaged in most companies. As with the culture of a company, context tends to be treated as a parameter, not a variable. Managers prefer to spend their time trying to change the person rather than the situation. They focus on "micro-managing" their people rather than "macro-managing" the work environment.

Likewise, in the so-called war for talent, time is invested in recruiting particularly gifted individuals – or at least those with the appropriate "competency profile" – rather than in creating an organisational context that engages the energies and enthusiasm of ordinary mortals.

People give of their best when their talents are fully engaged in their work. To be absorbed in a task that draws upon all one's

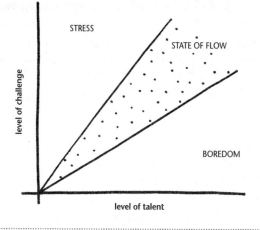

STRESS

STATE OF FLOW

level of challenge

BOREDOM

level of talent

Matching the task to the talent is fundamental to motivation

faculties is to be "in a state of flow" – a highly productive state of being. The danger signs in an organisation are when many people are either too stressed (the task exceeds the talent) or too bored (the talent exceeds the task).

Disengagement, from either stress or boredom, comes at a high cost. The skill of fully engaging employees in their work entails moving them from a purely instrumental relationship with their job, or from merely a contractual relationship with their employer, to a discretionary or voluntary relationship – one in which their work becomes intrinsically motivating. Management creates economic value when it designs an environment that earns the discretionary efforts of employees, particularly their creativity and courage, not simply their compliance and competency. For example, placing dissidents in positions of responsibility often propels them into a more positive, productive mode.

Percy Barnevik, a former CEO of ABB, has argued that it is a bad organisation that requires a great leader to run it. Peter Lynch, one of Fidelity's most illustrious fund managers, used to seek to invest in "simple businesses that anyone could run". Organisations that need managing brilliantly are simply organisations that are not serving a self-evident purpose, or are staffed with the wrong people, or are structured into jobs that require a high level of supervision. Wherever outstanding management is necessary, a fundamental error has been made in the design of the organisation.

Generally, managers are needed only because:

● people cannot do their job on their own without help and support (a problem of incompetence);
● people without close supervision would cheat on their employer (a problem of mistrust);
● the work to be done is ill-specified, the decision rights are unclear, or the customer is remote (a problem of ambiguity).

The same doubts and reservations about managerialism also hold for the concept of leadership, the more genteel word for management. "Stronger leadership" or "better leaders" is the fashionable battle cry, but why would a business ever want to employ someone who needed to be managed or led? And why would a self-respecting individual ever want to apply for a job that entailed being led by someone who was seeking followers?

Richard Rumelt suggests that, when times get tough, it is time to dispense with the people who need to be managed. But why wait for a recession?

Managers need to better exploit the benefits of heterarchy

"In a hierarchy, the top entrusts the understanding of detail to the lower levels, while the lower levels credit the top with understanding of the general, and so all are mutually deceived." **Karl Marx**

"Hierarchy works well in a stable environment." **Mary Douglas**

THERE IS A FAMOUS EXPERIMENT that demonstrates how collaborative organisations outperform hierarchies when it comes to solving complex problems. Five subjects sit round a table. They are separated from each other's sight by screens. Each of them receives six differently coloured marbles. Only one colour of marble is shared by everyone. The subject's task is to discover which colour it is. They can communicate but only by messages on index cards through slots in the screens.

There are three arrangements:

- the wheel, representing a standard bureaucratic hierarchy, where the messages are allowed to pass to only a single person, the "leader";
- the circle, representing a collaborative, egalitarian network, where the messages are allowed to pass between only immediate neighbours;
- the chain, representing an intermediary organisation, where the messages can flow in only one direction around the table.

The experiment ends when one of the players, confident of the solution, rolls the target marble down a tube to the centre of the table.

When the task is simple, such as when all the marbles are of the same colour, the wheel is the fastest, most efficient form of organisation. But when the task is trickier, such as when there is a wide variety of colours, the circle is the fastest and most accurate. The wider the channels of communication, the more efficient is the organisation, and the more engaged are the players. In the wheel, when it does well, only the leader takes pride in the result. In the circle, everyone feels involved and responsible.

As primates, we have a natural affinity with the alpha-male model of leadership. In our hunter-gatherer past, it served us well. But the tasks that the modern corporation is expected to solve are of a much higher order of complexity. Meredith Belbin, an expert on teamworking, suggests that, if we need a biological analogy, we should look to the "interdependent systems of social insects" for our models rather than to our own evolutionary past. He observes:

> Information is coming in from the side instead of top down ... By losing its likely monopoly on leadership, the top can survive with credibility only by empowering the most suitable individuals and teams.

The digital revolution, connecting everyone in an increasingly information-rich world, is dismantling the need for hierarchy and stimulating the development of new, more heterarchical organisational forms, appropriately called "lowerarchies".

⬤ Catalytic mechanisms point the way forward

....

"We need an implementation, as much as an innovation, engine."
Jeffrey Pfeffer

FOR A HIERARCHY, implementation is always problematic. How do you translate the heady visions and ambitious plans of senior management into results? How can the organisation be relied upon to deliver the intentions of its leaders with enthusiasm, precision and seamless co-ordination? The answer is usually a complex mix of instructions and controls. Because the whole process relies for its success upon the dutiful obedience and selfless goodwill of everyone in the organisation other than the leaders, it is little wonder that the results are so often disappointing.

For a heterarchy, problems of implementation are less acute if only because there is less of a divide between those who think and those who do. At W.L. Gore, a company best known for developing Gore-Tex fabrics, for example, people work only on projects that they themselves find inspiring, or, as Tom Malone describes it:

> To become a manager, you don't get promoted, you have to go out and find other employees who will agree to work with you ... you cultivate followership by selling yourself, articulating your ideas, and developing a reputation for seeing things through.

In this "democratic" setting, the task of seeing an idea through to completion does not distinguish between intention and action. Implementation ceases to be an issue. Nor does the task rely upon a power structure or a system of rules. Compliance and coercion are foreign concepts.

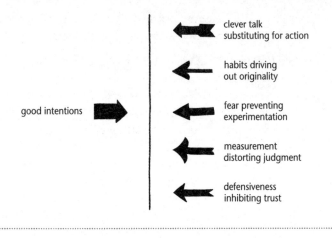

good intentions →

← clever talk
substituting for action

← habits driving
out originality

← fear preventing
experimentation

← measurement
distorting judgment

← defensiveness
inhibiting trust

An effective "implementation engine" would need more than "good intentions" to bridge the five causes of the "knowing-doing gap"

Source: Adapted from Jeffrey Pfeffer and Robert Sutton, *The Knowing-Doing Gap: How Smart Companies Turn Knowledge into Action*, Harvard Business School Press, 1999

Jim Collins has used the name "catalytic mechanism" (CM) to describe any managerial method that acts as "a galvanising, non-bureaucratic means to … translate lofty aspirations into concrete reality". He gives the example of Granite Rock, a small American company selling road building materials. Ambitious for greater success, the leadership team set the business a challenging goal: "to provide total customer satisfaction and achieve a reputation for service that meets or exceeds that of Nordstrom" (an admired North American retailer). But instead of embarking upon a bureaucratic quagmire of traditional mechanisms, such as town-hall meetings, road shows, service initiatives, black-belt awards, training courses, incentive programmes, and so on, a simple CM was invented, called "Short Pay". At the foot of every customer invoice, the following clause was added:

> If you are not satisfied for any reason, don't pay us for it. Simply scratch out the line item, write a brief note about the problem, and return a copy of this invoice along with your cheque for the balance.

Within two years, Granite Rock had won the coveted Baldrige Award, had increased market share and was charging a 6% price premium.

Most CMs work because they address directly the self-interest of all the stakeholders who need to be engaged in the project for it to succeed. They answer the question, "What's in for me?" There is no attempt to change opinions, alter attitudes or instil new beliefs. They dispense with the need to "get buy-in" or "get people on board" or "get everyone on the same page". They work because they are wholly aligned with the dominant motives, interests and desires of enough people to make the project work. They trade on the instincts of people to know their own interests and to act on them with enthusiasm. They run counter to everything normally associated with corporate-change programmes.

Above all, CMs are inherently heterarchical. They distribute power, compensate for the democratic deficit found in most companies, disintermediate levels of management, build and reward a sense of personal responsibility without the need for accountability, discover who are the natural leaders in the organisation, and inject the right measure of unpredictability into the system.

The message of CMs is that, faced with the need to raise corporate performance, the temptation to try to change people is a wasted emotion and a futile ambition. It is based on the conceit that other, less senior people in the organisation are less ambitious for success, or less capable of understanding what is in the firm's future interest, or less astute strategically. Most change programmes are experienced by those on "the receiving end" as insufferably patronising and condescending. The scope for altering other people to serve one's own purpose is extremely limited. Only under traumatic circumstances do people change. Seeking to change employees simply to fit the demands of the organisation is a far less productive strategy than changing the organisation to draw upon the aspirations and talents of the employees.

⬙ Everything important happens "at the edge of chaos"

....

"There ain't no rules around here. We're trying to accomplish something." **Thomas Edison**

"If you want to be productive, get disorganised." **Simon Caulkin**

ON A RECENT BUSINESS LEADERSHIP PROGRAMME, a senior executive at Rolls-Royce described two quite different internal cultures in the company, each triggered by a different set of circumstances: one (the "default" culture) was rational, structured, process-centric, rule-bound, risk-averse and compliant. The other, when there was a crisis of some sort, was emotional, spontaneous, problem-centric, improvisational, courageous and entrepreneurial. We have paraphrased his colourful description of how he and his colleagues in Rolls-Royce would "flip" from one behavioural style to another:

> When a crisis strikes and the reputation of the firm is at stake, we throw away the rulebook; we dispense with procedure; compliance loses its hold on us; and personal fear of failure ceases to cramp our style.

> We're no longer "managers" or "bosses" or "process owners" or "function heads"; we're problem-solvers, team players and human beings. We take our lead from the problem in hand, not from the command structure.

> Anyone who thinks he can contribute weighs in to help. Status, seniority and position lose their meaning. We become natural team players. No one stands on ceremony. We listen to – and build on – the ideas of others, we respect each other's thinking, and we invite customers and suppliers to join in, on the same terms.

> Everyone feels energised. We are "in the zone", wholly absorbed by
> the problem at hand and the common desire to solve it. We meet any
> place, any time, anywhere – whatever works best. We dispense with
> suits and ties – we wear what we feel comfortable in. We're just normal
> people, with our mates, bringing our skills together to solve a shared
> problem. We do whatever it takes.

The questions that exercised this executive were: Why can't this be
our standard way of working? Why can't we have the spirit of fire-
fighting without the need for a fire? How can we invent a surrogate
fire with the same heat but without the same collateral damage?

The deepest assumption that underpins much modern management practice is the idea that an efficient system needs a designer.
This notion is a variant of creationism.

Neither the theory nor the practice of management has begun
to grasp the full implications of the theories of evolution, or
complexity and the edge of chaos, or emergent order and self-
organising systems. Indeed, a degree of chaos may be the single,
and most important, missing element in the modern corporation. We are brought up to believe that every building needs an
architect, that every journey needs a destination, that every organisation needs an apex, that every task needs a goal, that every team
needs a leader and that every group needs a purpose.

However, these beliefs are by no means secure. We can have
co-ordination without a controller, as in the operation of the brain,
where no homunculus is required to direct mental activity; we can
have compliance without a regulator, as was once the case in the
City, where one's word was truly one's bond; we can have prediction without the need for prophets, as stockmarkets and betting
shops have taught us; we can have direction without a leader, as
exemplified in the flight of a flock of birds; we can have organisation without an architect, as the social life of insects demonstrates;
we can have design without a designer, as the origin of species and
the evolution of life forms prove; and we can have management
without managers, as the remarkable success of the world wide
web has shown.

🌑 Companies underestimate the power of intrinsic motivation

"Human beings have an inherent tendency to seek out novelty and challenges, to extend and exercise their capacities, to explore, and to learn." **Edward Deci**

"I have found in running businesses that the best results come from letting high-grade people work unencumbered." **Warren Buffett**

THE MAJORITY OF COMPANIES today rely heavily on systems of external rewards and punishments, such as short-term incentive plans and pay-for-performance schemes, to motivate their employees, despite mounting scientific evidence that financial motivators seldom produce the desired effect and, more often, actually harm performance.

Extrinsic motivation, which assumes that people respond positively to "carrots and sticks" by conscientiously raising their performance, has been shown to work only for routine tasks based on fairly simple rules – and then only for rather short periods of time before the incentive starts to wear thin. If the task demands imagination, ingenuity and improvisation, then financial incentives are far more likely to be counterproductive. They empty the work of its intrinsic pleasures and satisfactions. They demotivate the jobholder by implying that he or she has to be "bribed" to do a good job of work. In other words, employees see in these crude methods the assumption that they are naturally indolent and feckless, and only the fear of being punished or the greed of being "bonused" could ever shake them out of their torpor. Furthermore, the pressure to earn the incentive has been shown to have the effect of distracting or "rushing" the creative mind.

Because the workplace is becoming more and more skilled, the efficacy of extrinsic motivation is diminishing. The growing number of knowledge workers – and the rise of the creative class – means that more intrinsic forms of motivation are taking the place of rewards and punishments. Talented people are best motivated by the challenges and pleasures of the job itself – what Henry Royce used to call "pride in a job well done".

Recent psychological discoveries suggest that intrinsic motivation boils down to three main drivers:

- **Autonomy** – not to be the instrument of others' designs upon us but to be free to take responsibility for our own lives and to direct them in our own way.
- **Mastery** – not to find only toil in our work but to take pride in performing difficult and important tasks with greater and greater skill.
- **Connectedness** – not to be alienated from the world at large but to be serving a purpose more meaningful than our own self-interest.

The conditions most conducive to these qualities are those that promote the virtues of self-organisation as described in the experiment in the following essay.

❧ Tapping the collective intelligence of the organisation creates value

> "Conversations in the lavatory are more productive than those in the boardroom." **Russell Ackoff**

IMAGINE THE FOLLOWING SITUATION: You are an employee of a multi-divisional company. You work as a manager in one of these divisions. Suddenly, out of the blue, the board announces its decision to liquidate the company. You and every other employee, including the executive members of the board, are made redundant, but as compensation you are all given the exclusive right to bid against each other in a sealed auction for any of the company's assets in a month's time.

What would you do? How do you think your fellow employees would respond to this invitation? In particular, how many of you would go as far as assembling a bid and how would you spend the next month doing so?

We have described this thought experiment and put these questions to many different groups of executives attending many management-development programmes at London Business School over the past five years. The answers, from companies as diverse as Rio Tinto, BG, Roche, Danone, Deutsche Bank and Microsoft, are always remarkably alike.

Initially, people would form bidding teams. Individuals would seek out other individuals whom they knew and respected, whose companionship they valued, and whose talents they believed complemented their own. Once the teams were formed, they would identify an asset cluster in the business that from experience they were confident they could manage profitably. Typically, this would comprise a mix of intellectual property, such as patents, brand names, trademarks and research reports, and physical assets, such as buildings, plant and equipment. The precise mix would depend upon how each team interpreted its own distinctive competence and how they saw this combination of assets mapping onto future market opportunities. They would then price their chosen assets in the light of the strategy that they thought would work best; they would raise whatever capital they needed to make the acquisition; and finally they would tender their bid for the assets.

The outcome is as predictable as the process: roughly 5–10% of the employees of the company would hook up with one another in various team combinations. Many individuals would discover that they were not attractive to anybody else and were not being invited to join teams; others would find that their skills (and personality) were in huge demand. The reputation and perceived quality of individuals would bear no relationship to seniority, position or rank. The size of the teams that would emerge from such a process would average between five and seven people who, taken together, would bid for a selective subset of the assets of the business. In sum, these assets would be bought for 40–50% of the market value of the parent company. About one-third of the bidding teams would succeed in acquiring the assets they wanted; and of these, half would be out of business within two years; a further quarter would have been absorbed into other companies, some of them having merged with their former colleagues in other teams.

Predictions of future performance suggest that, within five years, the aggregate market capitalisation of this portfolio of surviving businesses would be at least double that of the legacy company at the time of its liquidation: for a company of 50,000 employees and valued at $5 billion, for example, these assumptions suggest that such an auction would split the company into 50 surviving businesses together worth $10 billion within five years.

Playing the auction game reveals some important truths.

The Pareto principle (the 80:20 rule) is alive and well

- It takes fewer than 10% of a typical workforce, freed from organisational constraints, to double, within five years, the value of an enterprise, using less than half of its balance sheet.

- Entrepreneurial skill or ambition seems to reside in few people – roughly 8% of the workforce.

- The bulk of a firm's assets are believed by most employees to be sterile and incapable of yielding positive returns.

Most large companies are unmanageable

- Considerable wealth is locked up in super-scale firms.

- Large companies are typically too complex to be managed effectively.

- The cause is less likely to be the incompetence of managers than the deficiencies of managerialism.

The modern workplace breeds disengagement

- Invited to contribute to the success of the enterprise, most employees, including the majority of managers, find it difficult to come up with ideas for radical performance improvement; they are not accustomed to wondering, "What would I do if I were the CEO or if I owned the business?"

- Most employees go to work to draw a salary or a wage rather than build an institution or create economic value.

- Only rarely does work call forth the requirement to be imaginative, to take a personal risk, to test an idea, or to explore the unknown.

Managerialism sets a low ceiling on performance

- The prevailing management model operates at about 50% efficiency. In other words, it leaves on the table about half the potential value of the enterprise.

- The knowledge of how to double the value of an enterprise certainly exists in the organisation – but it is dispersed among many minds and can be aggregated and applied only by an internal market.

- Executive boards that do not have access to this dispersed knowledge cannot be expected to make such well-judged strategic decisions.

Small changes of organisational context can liberate big improvements in corporate performance

Simply by offering greater freedom of choice and by placing greater trust in the judgments of large numbers of employees, a broad plethora of problems, whose solution is aggravated rather than enabled by traditional organisational methods, start to be skilfully addressed, such as:

- finding leaders;
- building teams;
- engaging employees;
- forecasting outcomes;
- pricing options;
- detecting waste;
- picking winners.

The smallest changes – if well chosen – can have the biggest effects

"Master the Fine Art of Nudgery." **Tom Peters**

ORGANISATIONAL CAPABILITY RESTS MAINLY on an understanding of how individual human behaviour can be crafted to be more effective. But what is known about why and how people change their behaviour?

Broadly, there are two traditions of thought. The dominant tradition, based on economic concepts of autonomic choice, rational deliberation and utility maximisation, focuses on the power of knowledge and the potency of self-interest. As a result, ways and means of influencing choice and changing behaviour have focused on the provision of crucial information and the creation of clear incentives. The assumption is that people cannot resist the power of an empirically grounded, logically coherent argument. This is the view of classical economics, as distilled in the notion of rational economic man, with its faith placed clearly in the power of cognitive reasoning.

The alternative, more recent tradition, noting that the choices made by real people often fail to live up to this rational standard, seeks instead to explain behaviour in terms of contextual factors, such as the choices made by others, and psychological biases, such as the aversion to risk. Focusing on concepts of judgment and bias rather than data and inferential logic, behavioural economists have discovered some startling truths about how human behaviour can be influenced by quite small adjustments in the immediate environment. The practice of this craft has been called "choice architecture".

For example, in California, dramatic reductions in domestic energy consumption were triggered simply when the invoices of utility companies were modified to include comparative household consumption data (without any accompanying judgment or admonishment). The greatest impact was among heavy users of energy whose average consumption, by being compared with that of their immediate neighbours, seemed "out of line", thus prompting them to consume less. This effect has been explained in terms of the normative bias, wherein most of us want to conform to our peer group.

Tom Peters has given the name "little BIG things" to these kinds of contextual triggers that "nudge" individuals towards more effective or responsible behaviour. He offers these three examples:

- Put geologists and geophysicists in the same room, and find more oil than your "separate room" competitors.
- Use a round table instead of a square table – and the percentage of people contributing to a conversation leaps up.
- If signing up to join a 401(k)-style tax-enhanced savings plan is the default option, 86% of people will join. If they must opt in, just 45% choose to join.

Richard Wiseman, a psychologist and writer, gives two further examples of "nudgery":

- People who visualise themselves taking the practical steps needed to achieve their goals are far more likely to succeed than those who simply fantasise about their dreams becoming a reality.
- Those who visualise themselves as others see them are about 20% more successful than those adopting a first-person view.

Using subtle contextual factors to shape behaviour has been called "paternalistic libertarianism" by Richard Thaler, an economist. To suggest that the most productive roles of managers in the future will be those of choice architect and paternalistic libertarian would seem to us to be a highly progressive move.

⬱ The spectre of bankruptcy serves to tame "animal spirits" more effectively than the restraints of the regulator

THERE ARE MANY ACTIVITIES that can be outsourced successfully by individuals, companies and governments. For example, individuals may choose to outsource the preparation of their tax returns to an accountant; many companies benefit from outsourcing the design and administration of their IT systems to a consultant; and governments are increasingly finding it more efficient to outsource the delivery of public services to voluntary organisations. Equally, there are some activities that cannot legitimately be outsourced. By definition, ethical responsibility for our own actions cannot be delegated, shared or outsourced. Moral accountability must attach to the author of the action.

Regulation has the perverse effect of encouraging those being regulated to outsource their conscience to the regulatory authority. For example, bankers have argued quite legitimately: "If something is not explicitly forbidden by the regulator, then it cannot be deemed irresponsible if we choose to adopt it or to practise it." By "socialising" moral responsibility and breaking the link between action and accountability, regulation reduces virtue to a tradable commodity. Replacing the personal fear and shame of bankruptcy with the institutional inconvenience of being fined or admonished by the regulator has taken the sting out of failure.

A morally mature society is one in which individuals are not just happy to take responsibility for their actions, but also recognise their obligation to be accountable to others for what they do. They want to be members of a society in which personal and corporate transgressions have personal and corporate consequences.

Taking responsibility for our actions includes learning conscientiously from our mistakes. One of the tragedies of the global economic downturn has been that the lessons of the debacle have not been learned. If no individuals see themselves as even partially responsible for the crisis, then no one has any reason to interrogate their own beliefs and values or make strenuous efforts to change their behaviour. Indeed, empirical studies of bankers in the City since the financial meltdown have shown that individual behaviour does not seem to have been affected at all by what happened.

We can learn from the health system. Recently, the European Working Time Directive (EWTD) has been widely blamed for encouraging junior doctors to desert the National Health Service, as well as having a malign influence on medical training, and for putting patients at risk. This is what David Nunn, a consultant surgeon at Guy's Hospital, had to say in a letter to the *Times*:

> Who is to blame for the nonsense that is now surgical training? Who accepted the changes introduced by Calman? Who agreed to allow nurses to take over the role of junior doctors to the detriment of both doctor and patient? Who acquiesced to the farrago of the Modernising Medical Careers programme? Who was persuaded to accept the "challenge" of redesigning training to meet the requirements of the EWTD? I am afraid it was me, and all of my senior surgical colleagues, who should have resisted all of the above. Not only have we failed the generation below us, but we have allowed politicians and managers to undermine our profession and our own status.

In the aftermath of the global economic downturn, who else has had Nunn's disarming humility to take any responsibility for what happened?

The economic costs of the banking crisis, however great, will always be trivial in comparison with the social costs of the regulatory methods designed to forestall them. It is better for a society to bear the costs of financial exuberance every 50 years or so, however painful, than suffer the decline in ethical standards, the abdication of personal responsibility and the depletion of social capital brought about by ever more intrusive, government-inspired regulation, however gradual. Sometimes in life, the therapy is more toxic than the disease it purports to cure.

🌀 Morality is not possible without the freedom afforded by the market

Antithesis: stakeholder theory

"In almost every corner of the earth, people are living longer and their lives are more prosperous, more pleasant and more peaceful. Capitalism – a much maligned beast in recent years – is coursing through the world, driving profound changes for the better, especially when allied to technological advances, urbanisation and good governance." **Ian Birrell**

EVEN THE SEVEREST CRITICS of capitalism recognise that markets have an extraordinary capacity to enrich the world. Wherever the combination of property rights, open capital markets, long-term funding and entrepreneurial activity has been found, the result has been an unparalleled growth in prosperity. Friedrich Hayek, an economist and Nobel laureate, even claimed that most people alive in the world today owe their very existence to the productivity that markets enable:

> We owe not only our prosperity, but our capacity to maintain a population as large as that to which the Western world has grown, to obeying certain traditional rules or morals, essentially the rules of property and family, whose functions we have never understood, which people dislike because they do not understand their function, and against which the great revolutionary movements of our time, socialism and communism, are directed.

Why, then, does capitalism get such a bad press? Why is it generally seen to be based on immoral motives, such as greed and selfishness, and to lead to immoral outcomes, such as materialism and

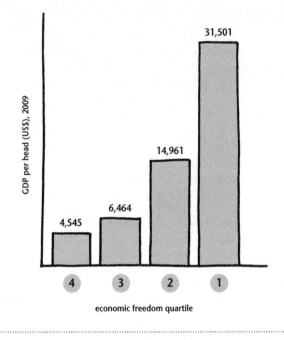

The relationship between national prosperity and economic freedom

Source: Fraser Institute, Economic Freedom of the World: 2011 Annual Report

inequality? Why do so many intellectuals affect to tolerate it but not to praise it?

First, those who berate the imperfections of capitalism point to the present-day gap between the rich and the poor as evidence of the malign effects of "the law of the jungle". But a fairer comparison would be between the poor of today and the averagely well-off in earlier times. Martin Wolf, an economics commentator, writes:

> All complex societies are unequal. In all societies people (generally men) seek power and authority over others. But, among sophisticated societies with an elaborate division of labour, societies with market economies have been the least unequal and the inequality they generate has been the least harmful.

In the things that really matter, such as living our lives as we choose and possessing the same legal rights as everyone else, capitalist societies are the most egalitarian in history. In a liberal democracy, no single individual, however wealthy or illustrious or powerful, exerts anything like the degree of influence over other people that is exerted by the ruling elite in an authoritarian society.

Second, those aspects of capitalism that people abhor are those aspects of human nature that are generally found to be unattractive. In other words, markets act as a mirror to the human race. The television programmes that people choose to watch, the newspapers that they choose to read, the retail stores that they choose to patronise and the merchandise that they choose to buy simply reflect the tastes and preferences of human beings. It is true that markets are much better at satisfying the needs and wants of the majority than the idiosyncratic desires of small minorities, just as they are much better at rewarding hard work and enterprise than, say, fostering the virtues of love and altruism. This is because markets, like democracy, place their trust in people to make their own choices in their own interests. Those who despair at the choices that ordinary mortals make under conditions of freedom are betraying their own disdainful attitude towards humanity as a whole.

Except where markets have enabled dominant suppliers to restrict choice and abuse their power, the profit motive is neither more nor less moral than the "wage motive" or the "price motive" or indeed the "happiness motive". In a market, each of us is trying to lead our own life in our own way – but without harming others' attempts to do likewise. Wanting the best for ourselves can be achieved in a market economy only by engaging with others in mutually beneficial transactions that also happen to serve their wanting the best for themselves.

Finally, without the economic freedom that only markets can create, morality is meaningless. If a choice is not freely made, it cannot be endowed with moral quality. Forcing people to be virtuous is neither virtuous in itself nor can its results be described as virtuous.

PART 4

Biases and remedies

....

WE ARE NOT THE FIRST MANAGEMENT SCEPTICS. There is a long history of cynicism towards the institution of management:

- Pareto's principle – a small proportion of people do most of the valuable work in any organisation.
- The Peter principle – everyone in an organisation is eventually promoted to their level of incompetence.
- Parkinson's law – work expands to fill the time available.

Appoint a manager and you can rest assured that he or she will be busy – however many managers you appoint. All too often it would seem that the preoccupation of managers is to invent managerial work, to look busy, to have a long list of things to do, to put the urgent ahead of the important and to give every appearance of being indispensable: the more managers there are, the more managers you need.

The 20th-century model of management was self-perpetuating:

- Design jobs that cannot be done without supervision.
- Fill them with people who are happy to take instructions.
- Set targets and design measures that keep people so busy

that they have no time to think.

- Emphasise speed.
- Reward managers for building empires.
- Encourage turf disputes to goad "performance".

Organisational cultures of "learned helplessness" developed in the wake of these principles. The time is long overdue not only for challenging the standard model of management but also for putting forward an alternative set of principles and practices that draw upon the new science of motivation and of complexity.

◈ New problems call for new methods

....
Transition: from more of the same to something different
....

"Without changing our patterns of thought, we will not be able to solve the problems we created with our current patterns of thought."
Albert Einstein

WHEN RICHARD FEYNMAN, a physicist, was asked what approach he used when trying to solve a particularly intractable problem, he recalled the methods that some of his forebears had used. He mentioned how Michael Faraday, a natural philosopher, formulated a model in his head, how James Maxwell, a physicist and mathematician, put equations together to formalise this model, how Paul Dirac, a theoretical physicist, got his answers by guessing an equation, how relativity theorists got their ideas by looking at principles of symmetry, and how Werner Heisenberg, another theoretical physicist, discovered his quantum mechanics by "thinking about only those things you can measure".

However, reflected Feynman, when the problem is fundamentally new, the tried and tested methods are no longer equal to the task:

> All that stuff is tried. When we're going against a problem we do all that. That's very useful. That's what we learnt in the physics classes, but the new problem, where we're stuck, we're stuck because all those methods don't work. So when we get stuck in a certain place, it's a place where history will not repeat herself. That's what makes it even more exciting. Whatever we're going to look at – the method … the trick … the way it's going to look – it's going to be very different from anything we've seen before. Therefore the history of

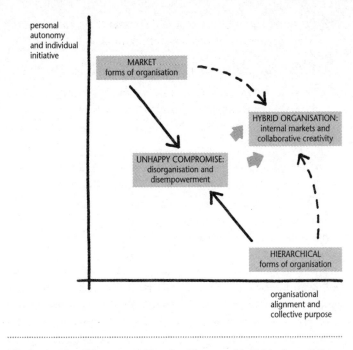

New ways of working: reconciling the dilemma of individual creativity versus organisational control

> the idea – of how things actually happened – is an accident. The only thing in physics is the experiment. History is fundamentally irrelevant.

(From an interview, published on the Feynman website, entitled "Take the world from another point of view".)

In business, we are at a point where the methods of traditional management have lost their efficacy. "We're stuck because all those methods don't work." The pace of environmental change is, perhaps for the first time in history, faster than our pace of learning. We urgently need to discover new tools for dealing with this higher level of complexity. The new web-based technologies are encouraging the growth of social networks and thematic communities around the world and contain the seeds of entirely new ways of engaging people, organising work and creating value. Over 4 billion people are now connected through wireless devices. Computers are no longer a luxury in much of the world. Information is virtually free. Soon, almost anyone in the world will be able to participate in global conversations on topics of their own choosing with people with similar interests and agendas.

The tools of collaborative creativity made available by the world wide web are creating a situation in which the individual rather than the task is becoming the focus of collective work. In the near future, companies may no longer be able to rely on imposed employment contracts and internal organisational structures to get work done. They will need to reach out to extended networks of gifted freelancers and find creative ways of engaging their talents if they are to remain competitive. On their own, companies will simply not have access to sufficient talent to innovate and survive. The critical competence of organisations will become their ability to earn their membership of highly creative networks critical to their own success – by contributing at least as much value to these communities as they receive. Skills of co-ordination and co-operation will become paramount. The performance bottleneck for many companies will not be their capacity to raise funds but their ability to join, build and sustain collaborative communities.

⟳ The logic of business decision-making should emulate the logic of scientific discovery

"We never argue from facts to theories, unless by way of refutation or 'falsification'. This view of science may be described as selective, as Darwinian. By contrast, theories of method which assert that we proceed by induction, or which stress verification (rather than falsification) … are typically Lamarckian: they stress instruction by the environment rather than selection by the environment." **Karl Popper**

THE PRINCIPAL ARGUMENT of this book is that profit is a return on knowledge and that therefore decision-making in business should be modelled on problem-solving in science, which is the most reliable and productive form of knowledge acquisition so far invented. Karl Popper treated the method of science as essentially the method of conjecture and refutation. Science progresses, makes discoveries and expands our knowledge by putting forward tentative and fallible models of reality, focusing particularly on structurally invariant patterns in the external world. It then tests these models impartially and rigorously. The role that science gives to nature is that of judge and jury in the evaluation of these models. Through experimentation, nature is forced to make its voice heard. In short, science proposes and nature disposes. What sets scientific thinking apart from pre-scientific thinking is that it seeks not to verify its theories, but to refute them.

Scientific inquiry starts with problems, such as beliefs that have failed us, or theories that have let us down, or more generally,

> "What gave you the idea of trying ...?"
>
> "I'm taking the view that ..."
>
> "What happens if you assume that ...?"
>
> "It follows from what you are saying that if ..., then ..."
>
> "Is that actually the case?"
>
> "That's a good question." (ie, about a true weakness)
>
> "That result squared with my hypothesis."
>
> "So obviously that idea was out."
>
> "My results don't make a story yet."
>
> "I don't seem to be getting anywhere."

....

Typical elements of scientific dialogue

Source: Adapted from Peter Medawar, *The Art of the Soluble*, Methuen & Co, 1967

expectations and predictions that have not been met. A problem has arisen which cannot be resolved with existing knowledge. A dogmatic attitude to such a situation would be to ignore it, or to deny it, or to fudge it. The scientific response is to explore it, to approach it from a different angle, and to try to resolve it. In place of dogmatism, science injects a healthy dose of critical inquiry. The result of this inquiry will be a variety of conjectural ideas formulated with a view to compensating for the deficiencies of the existing, erroneous belief system. These theories will inevitably compete with one another, each vying to provide the most satisfying solution. Science proceeds by discussing such theories critically, comparing their merits and their shortcomings. Popper has called this method "critical rationalism".

It is not an inductive process. Theories are neither summaries of facts nor distillations of observations. Scientists do not argue from facts to theories, except by showing that some of these facts falsify or refute some of these theories. Facts are used by scientists not as the source for their ideas but as the test of their ideas. What is called "knowledge" is simply the state of play in this critical discussion at any point in time.

In the same vein, we may say that our strategies, decisions and actions in business are rational if they are consistent with – or indeed inspired by – the outcome of critical inquiry. Whenever we have to make a decision, inevitably we will be comparing competing theories. Rationality means acting on the theory that has best withstood the robust attempts to falsify it. The mark of rational management is not just a tolerance of diversity of opinion and of robust debate but also an eagerness to root out falsehoods and a commitment to self-criticism.

Statements of corporate values trivialise ethics and demean employees

....
Transition: from values to virtue
....

"The de-moralisation of society is advanced when the word 'values' supplants the word 'virtues' in political and ethical contexts. When we move beyond talk of good and evil, when the categories virtue and vice are transcended, we are left with the thin gruel of values-talk."
George F. Will

NO ONE CAN DENY that corporate talk about "values" – along with the organisational effort that goes into writing and promulgating "value statements" – has increased dramatically over the last 20 years. It is equally self-evident, and perhaps paradoxical, that organisational behaviour is no more moral now than it was before this fashion for talking about it took hold. Indeed, we can perhaps discern an inverse relationship between the amount of time we spend talking about morality and the amount of effort we invest in behaving morally. As Ralph Waldo Emerson, an essayist, said: "The louder he talked of his honour, the faster we counted our spoons."

There has been a subtle shift in the use of the word "value". In earlier times, "value" was a singular noun meaning the worth of something. For example, we would talk about the value of certain forms of behaviour, such as co-operation or courage, or of certain classes of assets, such as companies and properties. But now it has become a plural noun. We ascribe "values" to individuals and organisations per se, as a way of summarising their beliefs,

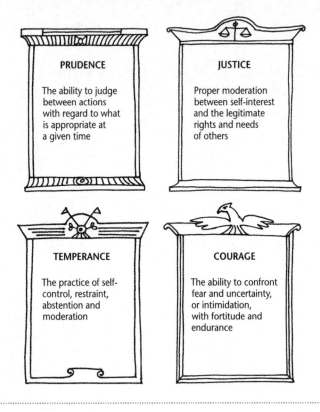

The cardinal virtues

Note: "Cardinal" derives from the Latin *cardo* or hinge; thus the cardinal virtues are the hinges upon which the door of the moral life opens and closes.

attitudes and dispositions. My values are contrasted with yours. One company's values are set against another's. We are assumed to choose our values rather as we choose our clothes. There is a market in values, a great assortment of choices. And each of us is encouraged to make a judicious choice of which ones we want to be judged by. We choose to define "worth" in our own unique way. In other words, values have been marketised, monetised, democratised and relativised. The moral moorings that value once possessed in the more absolute world of virtue have been lost.

When a firm selects its values, it is making as strategic a choice as when it selects which markets to address or which products to launch. With little reference to absolute standards or traditional morality, we construct our own subjective world of personal and organisational ethics. The only test then becomes its efficacy. If it advances our position, then presumably our values were skilfully chosen, and vice versa. Ethical positioning has become an element of a company's marketing mix.

Traditionally, virtue was not seen as a choice from a portfolio of options but as a hard-won habit. This is what made it rare, precious and praiseworthy. Virtues were practices acquired through diligence and humility. They were not lifestyle preferences or passing fads or means to an end. They were more akin to convictions, habits and duties.

The distinction between values and virtue is similar to that between personality and character. Just as we would be embarrassed to use the word "virtue" nowadays because of its ring of moral certainty, solidity and universality, so we find the word "character" an anachronism in the assessment of a person. We feel more comfortable judging a person's skills, especially if we couch them in the pseudo-scientific language of competency profiling; but we would be tempted to call it bigotry if someone were to judge an employee's character. Yet corporate performance almost certainly depends more on virtue than values, and more on character than personality.

Change programmes deliver greater change when focused on weakness of will rather than clarity of intent

Transition: from goals to rules

"Despite prolific output, the field of change management hasn't led to more successful change programmes." **McKinsey & Company, 2009**

IN MANY CHANGE PROGRAMMES, the assumption is made that most staff do not understand what is good for them and their organisations. Only when they can be persuaded to see the errors of their ways and be shown a clear vision for how things could be better will they resolve to make the necessary changes.

The vast majority of change programmes struggle because these assumptions are false. Many people in organisations can see that change would be beneficial and are open to being mobilised. Some are eager for change. Managers need to appreciate that attempts at forceful imposition will founder, and that they need to be collaborative. The trust they engender, their openness, the manifest authenticity of their purpose and will – and any number of other virtues – are essential if a firm is to improve its performance and to engage its staff.

One reason people do not always adhere to the noble admonitions and prescriptions of enlightened change programmes may be that the benefits of making changes are so remote and the costs so immediate that, for most managers and staff, it feels like an unfair deal. As with smokers, giving up their dangerous habit to prolong their lives has to be set against their immediate loss of pleasure.

The perseverance and strength of will required to get through the discomforts of the process to enjoy the full fruits of eventual success are rare in human beings. It takes only a minor setback or an easy temptation to weaken the will.

Anything that can serve to strengthen people's understanding, commitment and willpower is therefore good:

- **Rules rather than goals.** As with following a diet, success is best assured by adhering to a small number of strict everyday rules, rather than by simply signing up to a general principle.

- **"On the job" change rather than a free-standing initiative.** Change is not something done alongside "work as usual" but a different way of doing the everyday things.

- **Different measures.** If none of the performance measures is changed, no amount of proselytising will alter anything.

- **Different motives.** Change is motivated more by the fear of social embarrassment than by feelings of personal guilt.

- **Actions rather than words.** People take more notice of what their bosses do than of what they say.

- **Commitment rather than imposition.** People do not like being changed, but they will support changes they have helped to create.

- **Skin in the game.** If senior executives put their careers on the line – for example, by making their jobs and rewards contingent upon the success of the change programme – they will earn the trust of their people. Otherwise it is just posturing.

- **A matter of principle more than an expedient tactic.** People will sign up to change only if it possesses moral force – and is widely believed to be the right thing to do.

- **Loyalty to colleagues.** People will commit more because they don't want to let other people down than because it will help the bottom line.

- **Volunteers not conscripts.** People must join because they want to, not because they are coerced into doing so or because they fear the consequences of not doing so. They have to be part of the choice, made on their terms.

- **Choice of consequence.** Change is less about converting people and more about offering a choice and respecting the choice – of whether to commit or to leave – of every employee.

- **Little by little does the trick.** The principles driving the need for change may be long term; but the incentives and measures for tracking performance will need to be short term. Tracking daily progress, however modest, is the art of longer-term achievement.

🌐 Business is increasingly equated with being busy

"We typically and seemingly automatically solve our issues by adding more mechanisms." **Eric Abrahamson**

WE LIVE IN A WORLD where productivity is equated with urgency, speed, shorter lead times, faster cycle times – and the spirit of busy-ness generally. The call is for more of everything: more effort, more commitment, more initiative, more change. The Avis strapline, "We Try Harder", has become the implicit motto of management everywhere. Whenever there is a lull, there will always be someone who cannot bear the respite from frenetic activity and chooses to fill the silence with the noise and commotion of new demands, new challenges, new goals, new metrics and new incentives. Managers have become addicted to change. Organisations everywhere are awash with "change initiatives".

The British government under Tony Blair was famous for announcing initiatives that gave the impression of purposeful activity. Matthew Parris, a journalist and former politician, identified several types of these initiatives, or what he called "habits of displacement", including:

- **Reorganising departments** – "the political equivalent of that urge to hoover, repack, make coffee, move the furniture … which so often seizes those afflicted by frustration or anxiety".

- **Making appointments** – "tsars, supremos, ministers for

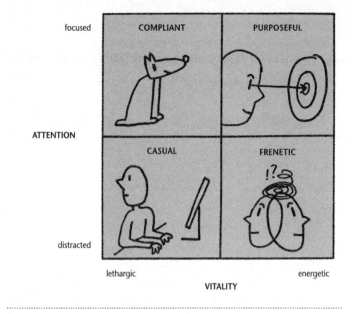

focused

COMPLIANT | PURPOSEFUL

ATTENTION

CASUAL | FRENETIC

distracted

lethargic | energetic

VITALITY

The pathology of the busy fool (bottom right): substituting displacement activity for purposeful behaviour

Source: Heike Bruch and Sumantra Ghoshal, "Beware the Busy Manager", *Harvard Business Review*, February 2002

children, task forces, as if the appointment itself was the 'delivery'".

- **Setting up commissions of inquiry** – "units set up to monitor, deliberate and report", a neat of way of kicking an embarrassing issue into the long grass.

- **Making unlikely promises** – "the unveiling of a plan, rather than its realisation, becomes the news … targets and mission statements are part of the same pathology".

The truth is that most companies would perform better with less organisation. We would do well to heed Adlai Stevenson's remark, when asked what his plans were should he win the American presidential election, "to bend every muscle to do as little possible".

There are greater returns on simplicity than on scale

"There seem to be many people making things more complex but very few people trying to make them simpler." **Edward de Bono**

SIMPLICITY HAS BEEN DEFINED by Edward de Bono, the originator of the term "lateral thinking", as "unification around a single purpose". It is rare because it is not natural. Simplicity is always the result of design.

To achieve simplicity, it has to be pursued doggedly. We often settle for the first solution we think of, rather than seek out a better or a simpler solution. When the first solution is too expensive, we go back to the drawing board. But we are less troubled when it is too complex. Perhaps we should be as worried by complexity as we are by cost.

Imagine the following thought experiment.

Companies take simplicity as seriously as quality. They promote the twin slogans "Simplicity is Free" and "Simple First Time". There is a corporate campaign for TSM (total simplicity management). Employees compete to become "Black Belts" in simplification. A group of employees is appointed to a "Simplicity Circle", which vets every new product and every new process for its simplicity. Teams are formed to simplify those that are deemed to be too complex. People are trained in the skills of simplification.

Would the benefits of TSM exceed the costs? Or is the "management of simplicity" a contradiction in terms – yet another of Matthew Parris's "habits of displacement"?

The cost of dealing with (needless) complexity is high. It is wise to assume that any process can be simplified without detriment. For example, parliamentary democracy is in desperate need of overhaul to make it more responsive, more efficient and more trustworthy. But many systems are not interrogated as they should be because they are taboo. For fear of making matters worse, people err on the conservative side of these debates.

It is an almost universal law that every business process becomes ever more complex as successive managers try to improve it by adding further functions and features. The corollary of this law is that those who operate the process do not notice the increasing complexity. It is also true that many people in an organisation have a vested interest in making things complicated and keeping them that way.

No one cuts costs by eliminating their own job. And yet who better to recognise waste than the culprit? But how can turkeys be made to vote for Christmas? The answer – only partly tongue-in-cheek – could be: reward those who create value by making their own jobs redundant – by continuing to pay at least part of their salary or, better still, by sharing the benefits equally between the organisation and the departing hero.

Progress results from wise insights rather than grand designs

WE LIVE IN AN AGE when brave aspirations and bold intentions are regarded as intrinsically heroic. Self-worth is assumed to be proportional to scale of ambition. Companies set "big, hairy, and audacious" goals. Governments resolve to "make poverty history" and to "reverse global warming". These intentions are stated without a trace of irony.

Big agendas are sometimes a symptom of small minds or, at least, managerial mindsets that, for want of understanding the details of the markets in which their companies are competing, prefer the banalities of vision statements, stretch goals and corporate missions.

Obedience to small rules can have a much bigger pay-off. George F. Will, a journalist, has argued that relatively modest changes in individual behaviour would have a much greater impact on long-term poverty in the United States than the government's policies of wealth redistribution and welfare provision. He expresses the change in the form of three small rules: graduate from high school; have no child out of wedlock; and have no child before you are 20.

Addressing the broader issue of poverty in the developing world, Hernando de Soto, an economist, has argued that the lack of an integrated system of property rights makes it impossible for the poor to leverage their currently informal ownerships into capital that, by serving as collateral for credit, would form the basis for an entrepreneurial society. One of his "small rules" for the alleviation of developing-world poverty is "give squatters in shanty towns legal title to the land they now live on", thereby "formalising" their informal capital.

In his 1977 annual report, Warren Buffett laid down four "small" investment rules to which he has adhered ever since: "Look for businesses that (1) we can understand, (2) with favourable long-term prospects, (3) operated by honest and competent people, and (4) available at a very attractive price." He quotes Thomas J. Watson senior, the founder of IBM, with approval: "I'm no genius. I'm smart in spots – but I stay around those spots".

Instead of dreaming up grand visions, stretch goals, strategic plans and heroic resolutions, a good question for any company is simply this: what are the four small rules that should guide our everyday practice?

🌀 Many strategic decisions would be better made by a plebiscite than by an elite

Transition: from reporting structures to internal markets

"But honestly, do you believe that 100 people each with $1,000 to invest independently would go more astray than a manager with a million dollar budget and a one-time decision to make?" **Gary Hamel**

COMPANIES SEEM TO BE BIASED against radical or discontinuous innovation in at least three ways:

- The range of investment options under consideration at any one time is typically drawn from much too narrow a spectrum, mainly because of a strong bias towards overprotection of the legacy business that brought the company its original success. For example, there is evidence from Conference Board research that diversification yields higher returns the further away a company moves from its core product-market position.

- In the absence of an efficient internal market, companies underprice their own resources, such as their talent, their internal funds available for investment and their physical assets. These biases give the incumbent managers of the legacy businesses first call on these resources at discounted prices (hence the fact that most subsidiaries would be more valuable as independent businesses than locked within the corporation to which they belong).

- Because individual creativity cannot be "commanded" into play, the nature of management sometimes has an intrinsic dampening effect on personal initiative and enthusiasm, with the result that the perseverance necessary to see an idea through to market success is rare and those in charge of such projects often resign in frustration.

The power of markets to stimulate entrepreneurship, while recognised at the macro level of inter-firm rivalry, is less likely to be advocated at the micro level of the firm itself. The competitive process, if applied within the firm itself, is usually rejected on the grounds that it would inhibit co-operation, ignite turf wars, harm co-ordination and inflict chaos upon the organisation.

Increasingly there is evidence that hybrid organisations, mixing elements of hierarchy and internal-market processes, are a viable option. For example, a British retail bank has been experimenting with an internal stockmarket as a way of rebalancing the resource allocation process away from a closed, rather secretive and elitist activity and towards a more open, democratic and pluralistic "conversation". In this case, competition, far from fragmenting the organisation, would seem to have achieved a level of co-ordinated decision-making greater than that which typically results from imposing upon the many a small number of key decisions made by the few. Chaos can be in the eye of the beholder. A strongly managed firm typically feels like an ordered society from the vantage point of those in command, but to those under their command, it can seem arbitrary, unpredictable and impulsive.

The two great virtues of the competitive process, as embodied in the market principle and as compared with hierarchical solutions, are first, that it radically expands the range of options under consideration (by bringing a far greater number and diversity of people into the process), and second, that it adjudicates between these ideas in a more egalitarian and democratic manner (by relying upon the collective wisdom of the crowd rather than the judgment of an elite).

🍃 Firms underestimate the collective wisdom of their employees

Transition: from expert knowledge to crowd wisdom

"If a group is smart enough to find a real expert, it's more than smart enough not to need one." **James Surowiecki**

THERE ARE SOME PROBLEMS that are clearly better solved by a crowd than by an expert: guessing the number of jellybeans in a glass jar, estimating the weight of a sow at a village fair, or betting on the outcome of a cup final. There are other problems that are better left to an expert: performing a triple bypass operation, piloting an Airbus 380, or playing Beethoven's *Hammerklavier* sonata. But what about the following tasks: forecasting the state of the economy in a year's time, predicting the outcome of the next election, choosing between alternative investment options, setting the price of a new product, selecting between alternative advertising campaigns, appointing the next CEO? Do these judgments call for expertise? Or would we be wiser to rely on the collective intelligence of a large number of reasonably well-informed, unbiased, engaged people? Should we pass the problem up or down, so to speak?

The bias in most organisations is in favour of expertise, or at least perceived expertise. The judgment of the crowd is felt to be suspect.

Crowds can be clever and wise – but they can also be stupid or mad. What accounts for the difference? For a crowd to be clever, it needs to be diverse in its membership, varied in its viewpoints, free from coercion and unstructured. There must be no leadership, no power structure, no opportunities for contagion or collusion, no groupthink, no pressures to conform and no fears or favours in respect of outcomes. The individuals that comprise a wise crowd need to feel free to express their individual opinions, to be independent of the opinions of others in the crowd, and to be happy to be in a minority.

Accordingly, an organisation, such as a firm, can never be a clever crowd in so far as its members are encouraged to share a common set of goals, sign up to a common set of values, interact frequently with one another, influence each other's thinking, place a high value on unanimity, be prepared to compromise, take their cue from the leadership, take care not to depart too far from the party line, play as a team and work to diminish their differences. These values, so precious if the main aim is to sustain the status quo, become actively obstructive if the goal is to reinvent the business, pioneer new business models, or invent new markets.

Crowds become foolish or deluded or dangerous when they are led by charismatic leaders, or when they abandon their independence of mind, or when they are fixated on the opinions of others, or when they are over-impressed by the majority viewpoint or the zeitgeist or fashionable opinion.

People in a crowd are at their best – particularly as problem-solvers – when they choose not to communicate with each other. In other words, each of us contributes most to collective decision-making when we act wholly in line with our own beliefs. Only then is the average opinion of a crowd superior to the considered opinion of an elite.

The kinds of problems that lend themselves to collective intelligence are cognitive problems, where the answer is either right or wrong, such as forecasting next year's sales, or promoting the best person for the job, or choosing between strategic options, or pricing a takeover target, or predicting the response of a competitor, or foreseeing the outcome of a decision. This does not mean consensus. It is simply the "average opinion" of the group, however much the group may be in disagreement.

The growth crisis in large companies that Adrian Slywotzky, a consultant and writer, has documented is not the result of an absence of imaginative ideas, or a shortage of creative talent, or a lack of critical information, but rather a lack of effort to mobilise the wisdom of the organisation, or worse, a lack of desire to do so. The information and ideas sufficient to address the crisis are already in the minds of the employees, but the process for capturing and summarising this intelligence is absent.

Firms would benefit from becoming more open societies

SEVERAL EMERGENT FORCES are encouraging greater democratisation of the workplace. Increasing numbers of better educated, more ambitious, less deferential and more assertive "knowledge workers" are entering the market. There is a discernible shift towards the values of self-expression, collective creativity, inclusiveness and authenticity. The egalitarian language of rights, as a counterweight to organisational notions of personal accountability, has become part of the corporate lexicon. Firms find themselves having to compete to be perceived as "employers of choice". Managerial prerogatives, sometimes referred to as "bossism", are being challenged. There is greater cynicism towards figures of authority and less trust in institutional power than ever before. In this context, we should not be surprised if arguments for greater corporate democracy are finding favour among young managers and their more enlightened bosses.

Russell Ackoff was one of the first organisational theorists to put forward an operating model of what he chose to call a "democratic hierarchy". He argued for three core principles:

- Everyone has a right to participate in the making of those decisions that will significantly affect them.
- Everyone has a right to do whatever they want to do, subject to not harming the interests of anyone else.
- Everyone has a right to exercise, jointly with their peers, collective authority over those to whom they report.

Starting with the familiar organisation chart, each manager has his own job. For this organisation to count as democratic, Ackoff suggested that no manager should be allowed to make a decision without the agreement of his "board", where each manager's board consists of a minimum of three people: his boss, an immediate subordinate and himself. The board can, of its own accord, choose to expand its membership to include as many people as it wants, provided that no stakeholder group outnumbers the subordinate group. These added members can be drawn from any source, inside or outside the organisation. All the key decisions in the organisation are made by boards, not individuals. All board decisions are made by consensus.

Following Ackoff, each board has the same discrete set of responsibilities:

- plan the activities of the individual whose board it is;
- define what consensual decision-making means in practice;
- select its own members over and above the core trio;
- choose its own working methods and rules of engagement;
- align its own plans with those made one level below and one level above;
- ensure that each manager routinely asks their subordinates what they could do differently to raise their performance – and vice versa;
- exercise the right to remove a manager whom it deems unsuitable to the task.

Democratic processes have huge philosophical and ideological appeal to people of good will. Yet most business organisations fall well short of operating in accordance with these principles.

⬤ Most of the important things are happening at the periphery

RALPH STACEY, a management scholar, describes organisations as positioned in a two-dimensional space, where the axes are agreement and certainty. A high level of agreement would describe an organisation that is unanimous on most of the decisions for dealing with the critical issues that it is facing. A high level of certainty would describe an organisation that possesses good predictive knowledge of the outcome of any decision it might make. An organisation that is far from agreement has failed to establish a consensus on where the issues lie or on what its goals should be or on where its priorities are. An organisation that is far from certainty lacks the experience to connect cause and effect in what it does with any degree of reliability or confidence.

The standard management model defined in Part 3 is well fitted to a steady-state situation where agreement is easy and certainty is justified. In this case, it is perfectly rational to gather data, make predictions, set targets, build plans, agree budgets, monitor performance and reward success. Managers understand these conditions and have the tools to manage them predictably and effectively. It is only when the conditions do not lend themselves either to an easy consensus or to 20:20 foresight that the management model betrays its frailty.

In these circumstances, managers, desperate at least to feel in control, use various ploys and conceits to persuade themselves

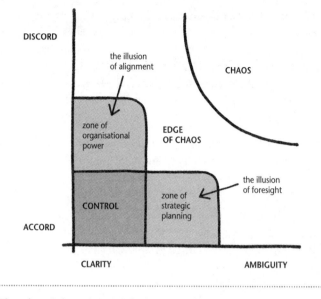

The edge of chaos: beyond the limits of planning and control

Source: Adapted from Ralph Stacey, *Complexity and Creativity in Organizations*, Berrett-Koehler, 1996

that the situation is controllable. They design elaborate strategic planning processes to pretend that the future is predictable and to provide at least a sense of certainty. They build command and control structures to amplify their voice, to extend their influence and to create some sense of shared purpose and agreed agenda.

Stacey argues that managers deceive themselves if they place faith in structures and systems to provide, in all circumstances, the agreement and certainty that they crave. The situation facing the firm may be too new, or too difficult, or too turbulent to be managed in the traditional manner. Under these conditions, managers need to place trust in the fact that complex systems have an extraordinary ability to be self-organising. Order emerges naturally from interactions within the network. By trusting in the emergent properties of loosely coupled networks, managers do not need to feel that they are surrendering their organisation to anarchy and chaos. They are, in effect, using the natural properties of networks to steer the organisation towards a state between total predictability and total disorder. This is the zone that Stacey calls "the edge of chaos". It is where creativity, invention and innovation flourish. A firm that cannot access this "flow state" is denying itself the level of risk and the state of "messiness" that is required if it is to create value.

Management is the skill of placing the firm in this messy, semi-chaotic, yet highly productive zone and holding it there. This skill requires a broader portfolio of managerial models than the standard version.

⬛ A sense of fairness is the glue that holds an organisation together

Transition: from power play to fair process

WHY SHOULD ANYONE COMMIT to a collective decision that goes against their convictions as to what is the right decision? How do people stay loyal to an organisation that sometimes (and inevitably) makes decisions directly contrary to their best judgment? For an organisation to work – and to succeed – it needs to acquire the art of making collective decisions in a way that earns the trust and loyalty of all its members.

Trust is the glue of an organisation. Trust in a manager is earned more by the fairness of the process he or she uses to reach decisions than by anything else, including the quality of the decisions themselves. If the process is seen to be autocratic or arbitrary or capricious, then the trust placed in the manager – and in the quality of the decision – will be low. But if the process is seen to be open, inclusive, rational and, above all, fair, then the manager will earn the trust of the team and of others. If managers are to engage the creativity of their people, they must be seen to be advocates of – and adherents to – fair process.

What makes a decision-making process fair? How do managers assess the fairness of a process? Studies show that, for the majority of people, three conditions need to be present to create a sense of fairness:

- **Participation.** Anyone who is affected by the outcome of a decision feels that they have a right to be involved in the process of reaching the decision. Involvement means not just contributing ideas and options but also challenging the ideas and options of others – without fear of reprisal. Participation does not necessarily entail making the final decision – or even having a vote – but it does mean the right to have one's views heard, understood and discussed. Only when people feel that the process has given their ideas an equal right to be taken fully into account will they give their blessing to the outcome of the process, irrespective of which decision comes out of it.

- **Transparency.** Anyone who is part of the decision-making process feels that they have a right to know why the decision to which it led was made. The test is not whether they agree with every step of the argument, but whether the process is sufficiently transparent for them to fully understand the reasoning that led to the decision. This strengthens their belief that the process is open, impartial and rational. By closing the feedback loop, it also serves to promote the importance of learning from others – and from experience.

- **Equity.** Anyone who is bound by the consequences of a decision has the right to equal treatment under the new "rules of the game". This means that everyone who is subject to the rules understands them – including the expectations, standards and criteria implied by them – and is confident that these will be applied equally to all.

A process is fair not because it arrives at a consensus or expresses the view of the majority or accommodates everyone's interests, but because it honours these three principles.

The pace of progress would be accelerated by greater corporate disclosure

"When in doubt, let it out." **Warren Bennis**

"Sunlight is the best of disinfectants." **Louis Brandeis**

TOTAL TRANSPARENCY is neither desirable nor feasible. Organisations have a right to secrecy when it is in the interest of fair competition. Intellectual property, for example, is legitimately protected by patent and copyright law. Issues arise when companies keep secrets for no other reason than to save face or to conceal error. Warren Bennis, a pioneer in the study of leadership, has observed that, "unfortunately, the reflex reaction in most companies is to treat all potentially embarrassing information as the equivalent of a state secret".

The case for transparency is that it is the simplest and cheapest antidote to the abuse of power. A company that runs on secrecy, confidentiality and fear is one that hoards information, conceals bad news, encourages groupthink and censors dissent. Even the act of questioning a decision is regarded as disloyalty. When leaders deliberately set out to support transparency, openness and candour, the results can be startling.

Tom Stewart, a professor at Harvard Business School, has become one of the most powerful advocates of transparency, particularly in relation to executive compensation. The Danish government, in line with this thinking, is currently experimenting with laws that would demand full disclosure, in plain language, of every-one's salaries, including bonuses, stock options and other "extras". Stewart has pointed out that, until the 1920s, American corpor-ations were not required to publish their sales revenues as part of their annual report and accounts. When, in the mid-1920s, they were legally forced to do so, there was widespread dismay within the ranks of senior management. By what principle, they argued, did anyone outside the company have the right to know the value of its sales – and therefore its market share and its competitive performance? Wasn't this a gross and unwarranted invasion of corporate privacy? However, by common consent, the effect was to make markets more efficient as the comparative performance of companies became more visible and therefore more interpret-able. Companies could now learn from each other's successes and failures.

Why shouldn't companies be required to report on the returns on their human capital as well as their financial capital? Stewart has argued that the greatest flaw in modern organisations is the difficulty they have in making change happen. His remedy is radically greater corporate transparency, starting with pay: the more that people know, the greater the pace of organisational change. Innovative practices that add value but are often under-estimated by senior management, such as self-managing teams, would gain faster acceptance and wider adoption. Experimental outcomes – whether intended or accidental – would gain greater traction. Letting light into the darker corners of the organisation would expose misallocation of resources, unfair decisions, abuses of power and improper practices.

Visualising the connection between decisions and outcomes enhances the quality of management

Transition: from invisibility to visibility

THE VALUE OF TRANSPARENCY in business is exemplified by "Work-Out", the celebrated process of open and candid conversation mandated during Jack Welch's leadership of GE. By encouraging and rewarding people at all levels to voice their opinions and ideas in the presence of their bosses and peers in large open meetings, the organisational capacity for managing change and the responsibility that people took upon themselves to push through change were dramatically increased. Of all Welch's initiatives, this is the one that made the greatest impact and will be remembered longest.

In building a culture of candour and transparency, managers have a responsibility to do certain things that do not come naturally in the workplace:

- **Straight talk.** Tell people what they need to hear in preference to what they want to hear, thus encouraging others to do likewise.

- **Fearless talk.** Create the conditions for people to prefer to share their knowledge, however discomforting, than to conceal it.

- **Contrarian talk.** Encourage people to play the role of devil's advocate, recognising that innovation invariably entails the inversion of standard thinking.

- **Awkward talk.** Recognise – and seize – the moment when difficult conversations about difficult topics with difficult people can best be broached.
- **Plural talk.** Multiply the perspectives represented in the corporate conversation, with a view to balancing everyone's biases.

Organisational learning depends more than anything upon people seeing the consequences of their action. This effect is amplified when everyone's actions are made visible to everyone else in the organisation. The power of "deutero-learning" – learning from the experiences of others – is a powerful but underutilised tool of management.

People are wired to learn. There is a strong instinct to make sense of everything that we observe. The more we see, the more we learn. In particular, we would change our behaviour more freely if we saw enough evidence of different ways of behaving that demonstrably worked well. An important role of managers should be to act as "makers of meaning" – publicly interpreting anything that the organisation finds surprising, novel, unfamiliar, ambiguous or confusing.

We use the phrase "accounting" far too narrowly in business. To "give an account" of a particular phenomenon should mean more than describing it financially. It should mean providing a well-reasoned explanatory account of what happened, and why. Every decision leaves a trace. Making visible the traces of everyone's behaviour helps the organisation to see itself "in the round", to interpret what is happening, to connect causes with effects, and to learn from the collective experience of all. It closes the feedback loop. Not only does it facilitate collective learning but, by helping everyone to see the impact of their actions, it enriches the workplace and gives people a highly motivating sense of their own contribution to the total result.

A parallel to this is the importance of "visualisation" in lean manufacturing. If you can see the work-in-progress inventory to which you, as an operator, are inadvertently adding, you are more likely to take steps to reduce it than if that same inventory were simply a line item on a set of management accounts.

All progress emanates from the freedom to make mistakes in the pursuit of organisational learning

....

Transition: from diktat to experimentation
....

CAPITAL ONE, the fifth most valuable credit card in the United States, came late into the market and built its success on the back of thousands of experiments, testing seemingly infinite variations on ways of designing, marketing, pricing, communicating, targeting, promoting and cross-selling its credit card. In this respect alone, Capital One is an unusual business. The randomised testing of business ideas or management practices, using test and control groups, has a long and distinguished history in R&D laboratories but is rather rare in other departments of companies.

It is commonly observed that many critical decisions made by executives are based on flimsy evidence. Even the assumptions upon which the rationality of these decisions is based are rarely spelt out in a manner that invites debate. Experimentation is typically regarded as an expensive, laborious, time-wasting and ultimately inconclusive way of settling differences of opinion. Firms prefer to rely on intuition, or common sense, or majority opinion, or what Hal Varian, a professor at the University of California at Berkeley, has called a "HIPPO" (a highly paid person's opinion).

At lower levels in an organisation, when managers disagree on a course of action, it is rare for both sides of the argument to settle their differences of opinion through a carefully designed and impartial test. Typically, the problem is escalated to a senior

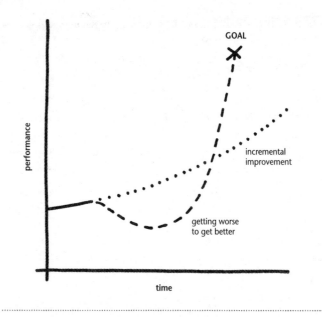

Two routes to the same goal: incremental improvement (optimisation)
or discontinuous change (*reculer pour mieux sauter*)

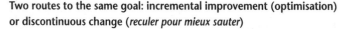

executive for arbitration, or there is a fudged compromise, or one
side of the argument backs down, or the strongest voice wins out.
Managers bow to the power structure rather than the truth to
break the deadlock.

The reluctance to experiment is part of a more general malaise
that might be called "the fear of slowing down – or even going
backwards". Every corporate success contains the seeds of its own
demise. The world changes and suddenly what once seemed so
perfect now seems ill-fitted to its environment. The problem is that
management is understandably reluctant to go backwards in order
to go forwards. For managers it goes against the grain to make
their organisations worse on purpose, even if it means getting
better at things in the long run. Markets too make it difficult for
companies to become less perfect so as to become more fit. But

the truth is that the next leap forward first requires a measure of "unlearning". Experimentation is always a brave investment in waste, inefficiency and temporary confusion and is the only sure way of tackling the next peak beyond the valley.

Capitalism has been defined by William Baumol as "a round-about process": fishermen, for example, take time out from fishing to invest their time, imagination and income in bigger, more productive boats. Experimentation is also a round-about process. It's a case of slowing down now in order to speed up later.

◓ Conversations, rather than meetings, are the units of organisational effectiveness

···
Transition: from control to conversation
···

> "To be a catalyst is the ambition most appropriate for those who see the world as being in constant change, and who, without thinking that they can control it, wish to influence its direction." **Theodore Zeldin**

IT HAS BECOME A WIDELY HELD and unchallenged axiom that all change has its origins in one of two processes: at one extreme, change is seen to be the product of the individual genius, the person of vision, the charismatic leader, or the heroic revolutionary; at the other extreme, change is modelled as the inevitable outcome of the tide of history, or of invisible economic forces, or of technological breakthroughs, or of large-scale democratic shifts. These are both rather demeaning and dehumanising viewpoints. Individuals get caught up in forces that are larger and stronger than them: in other words, change is created only by great individuals or mass movements.

Theodore Zeldin, a historian of ideas, has proposed a much more hopeful view: people change themselves as a result of personal encounters with people of varied views and experiences. In the search for companionship, and in conversations with others, we find a direction for ourselves. We complete ourselves by absorbing something of others. When people meet there is always the possibility of something new happening. As with science, it is the mixing of previously unrelated ideas and frames of reference that ignites new ideas and discoveries.

What holds us back is fear, timidity, aversion to what is unfamiliar, unpredictable, or uncontrollable. Only in losing control and surrendering ourselves to curiosity do we give ourselves the opportunity to grow, to discover and to change. The ideal situation in which to tame these fears and anxieties and to place ourselves at the centre of change is the privacy of a small-scale conversation where the parties treat each other with respect, as equals in the larger project of the organisation of which they are members. This is made difficult at work because life in an organisation has a habit of turning every conversation into a meeting with an agenda, or a project with a goal, or an initiative with a sponsor. Because a good conversation has no destination, it is more likely to arrive at an interesting and unexpected place. Conversations work best when they cross boundaries: addressing unusual questions, taking place in unfamiliar venues, or mixing different disciplines.

For a conversation to be productive, it needs to be more than exchanging information, gossiping, or passing the time agreeably. Trust is developed, tested and reinforced by participants being open to their real feelings, hopes, anxieties, experiences and deeper thoughts. Only by self-revelation does the potential for creativity and discovery take hold.

Conversation is the most potent instrument of change, if only because mindsets become particularly malleable in the context of strong personal relationships and their associated conversations.

Good conversation is founded upon good manners

"As civilised human beings, we are the inheritors, neither of an inquiry about ourselves and the world, nor of an accumulating body of information, but of a conversation, begun in the primeval forests and extended and made more articulate in the course of centuries ... it is the ability to participate in this conversation, not the ability to reason cogently, to make discoveries about the world, or to contrive a better world, which distinguishes the human being from the animal and the civilised man from the barbarian. Indeed, it seems not improbable that it was the engagement in this conversation (where talk is without conclusion) that gave us our present appearance, man being descended from a race of apes who sat in talk so long and so late that they wore out their tails." **Michael Oakeshott**

IN HIS ESSAY "ON DUTIES", Cicero was the first major writer to lay out the principles and skills of good conversation: speak clearly; speak naturally but not for too long; notice when others want to speak; take it in turns; do not interrupt; be polite; deal conscientiously with serious matters but lightly with frivolous ones; do not speak ill of anyone behind their back; keep to topics of general interest; refrain from talking about yourself; and never lose your temper. Later generations added more rules: remember people's names, be an attentive listener, and avoid giving the conversation a purpose outside itself, or over and above the pleasure of partaking in it.

Dr Johnson defined conversation as "talk beyond that which is necessary to the purposes of actual business", and Michael

Oakeshott, a philosopher, expanded on this important idea when he suggested:

> Conversation is not an enterprise designed to yield an extrinsic profit, a contest where a winner gets a prize, nor is it an activity of exegesis; it is an unrehearsed intellectual adventure.

It is in conversation that we learn the skills of empathy, of mutual respect, of building relationships of trust and equality. Conversation rewards the rare skill of listening.

A good conversation is a model of the kind of relationship that is generative, productive and fruitful. It sets a standard of what productive work in an ideal world would look like and feel like. It is the smallest, yet most potent, unit of interaction out of which great organisations are built. Indeed, an organisation is perhaps no more than the sum of the conversations that take place within it or are inspired by it.

Businesses therefore should give themselves the remit to create forums in which people with different and complementary talents find it easy and natural to converse.

⬢ Listening without judging creates the context for organisational learning

"Seek first to understand, then to be understood." Steven Covey

LEADERS HAVE MUCH TO LEARN from therapists and, in particular, from the work of Carl Rogers, the founder of "non-directive counselling", also called "client-centred therapy". Rogers became famous in the 1950s by challenging the prevailing assumption of both behaviourism and psychoanalysis that "the therapist knows best". He argued strongly against this presumptive model. In his own therapeutic practice, he refrained entirely from giving advice, or offering suggestions, or indeed anything that could be interpreted as persuasion, direction, control or inducement. Instead, he showed that it was the attitude of therapist towards client and the relationship between therapist and client that were much more important in effecting a cure than the therapist's theoretical knowledge or technical know-how. He was convinced that people are perfectly capable of directing their own lives and solving their own problems, provided that they perceive themselves to be in a climate of respect and trust. Thus the role of the therapist is to create just such a climate.

Rogers believed that a climate of respect and trust is characterised by three critical elements:

● **Congruence of thought, feeling and behaviour.** The therapist, if he is to be himself in the presence of the client, must discard any artificial facade that conveys the notion of a role being played or a persona being adopted. This may entail a certain degree of self-disclosure on the part of the therapist. Whatever makes him human, real and genuine is valuable to the therapy.

- **Unconditional positive regard.** The greater the amount of non-possessive care shown by the therapist, expressed in terms of non-judgmental acceptance of the client's thoughts, feelings and behaviour, the greater the chances of therapeutic success. Listening without judging is the essential skill.

- **Accurate empathic understanding.** The task facing the therapist is to build a deep enough understanding of the client's subjective world to be able to "see through their eyes". Sometimes called "decentering", this is the skill that comes from attentive listening and that puts in place the trust that enables the client to become less guarded and to take more responsibility for their own development.

The importance of these three conditions is that, if they are met, the responsibility for the therapeutic process moves from the therapist to the client. As the client becomes more open to his own experience, more trusting of his own ability, more confident in his own answers, and more willing to set his own agenda, so he becomes more able to deal with reality, to chart his own course and to grow on his own terms. The therapist is not trying to get his client to change or to follow a particular course of treatment or to accept his professional advice or indeed to do anything. Through the human qualities of the relationship, he is drawing upon every person's natural ability and resourcefulness to know what is best for them and what is the right path to growth, health and happiness.

Rogers himself said:

> If I can provide a certain type of relationship, the other person will discover within himself the capacity to use that relationship for growth and change, and personal development will occur.

Indeed, he went further and claimed that "significant positive personality change does not occur except in a relationship". These theories, if we were to adopt them conscientiously in corporate life, would have powerful implications for how leaders lead and how change is managed. By emulating the core skills of attentive listening, mutual respect and decentering, organisational capability would be transformed for the better.

Leaders who led in a Rogerian way would be adopting the following principles:

- Suspending their own expertise (and egotism) in order to build a non-judgmental relationship with others.

- Listening to others with sufficient empathy for them to feel – and know – that they have been heard and understood.

- Adopting the other's internal frame of reference and thereby opening up the possibility of "real" conversation, and a genuine meeting of minds.

- Using – and deepening – the growing level of trust so as to have ever more open and difficult conversations designed to enhance self-understanding.

- Entering into these conversations in the spirit of curiosity rather than judgment.

- Acknowledging that they cannot be – and should not want or need to be – in control of other people.

- Recognising that by surrendering the notion of control, they are opening up the possibility of much greater influence and power.

⮞ Learning how to learn more effectively is the challenge of our times

> "The interesting 'stuff' usually is going on beyond the margins of the professional's ever-narrowing line of sight." **Tom Peters**

WE ARE THE HEIRS to a view of learning and innovation that, in the age of the internet, has become, if not obsolete, then certainly outmoded. The idea that great ideas come from great individuals working alone is part of the mythology. When we think of innovation, the images that come to mind are the lone genius, the boffin, the artist in a garret, and the crank.

We divide the world into two, virtually discrete parts: the creative world of special, if not eccentric and unmanageable people responsible for having ideas, inventing products, generating solutions; and ordinary mortals who take these inventions to market. In business, we think of the R&D lab, set in isolation, with its own culture, far away from the cut and thrust of day-to-day business. The only link between lab and factory is the one-way pipeline through which new products are dispatched to operations and sales – and ultimately to users. If we need faster growth, or greater creativity, or a new family of products, we look to greater numbers of these special people to provide them.

The pipeline model of invention-driven innovation is in decline. "Blockbusters", whether in pharmaceuticals or other industries, are getting rarer. Escalating development costs, riskier returns, shorter product life cycles and cleverer competition mean that innovation is under huge pressure. People are looking for alternatives to the closed, specialist, seemingly unmanageable, pipeline model of innovation.

One way is to move towards a more open, more inclusive, less specialist process, as the internet makes the "tools of collaborative creativity" available to all. Open-source communities are just one of many new organisational forms that are changing the face of innovation and entrepreneurship. Innovation is becoming something much closer to a mass activity. Almost instant and free access to information and knowledge, combined with the ease and cheapness of communicating globally, have meant that investment in libraries and labs is no longer the only ticket to innovation. We can now talk of "mass innovation".

Small companies – and the BRIC (Brazil, Russia, India, China) economies – are taking a bigger and bigger share of the R&D load. Open innovation models, collaborative creativity on the net, application of the new social media to problems of invention and innovation are all coming into their own. More global, more "amateur", more voluntary, more multi-disciplinary, more communitarian models for how new products and services are brought to market are being developed.

Big companies are seeking ways to tap into these new methods and communities, co-opting the experience and imagination of customers to co-invent the next generation of products; creative communities themselves are struggling to monetise their business models without being absorbed into corporations.

PART 5

Applications and examples

PRACTICAL METHODS of redressing organisational bias, especially the bias in favour of control at the expense of learning, are essential if strategic thinking is to be strengthened and managerialism is to be reformed. Reprising the double-loop diagram from Part 3, this final section puts forward a model of organisational capability that has the power to shift the locus of the firm to the right loop centred on learning and discovery.

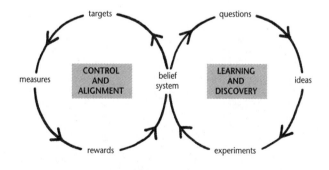

The two vital loops: combining the virtues of alignment and discovery

Most corporate work goes on in the left loop: the domain of control and of keeping things going; of grinding out efficiency gains; of doing more of what we already do; of continuous improvement and making all those minor adjustments that tweak the effectiveness of existing products and processes. By contrast, what we call the discovery process focuses unequivocally on the right loop: the domain of experimentation; of expanding the range of fresh insights; of reflecting on existing habits and assumptions; of aspiring to new wisdom and more compelling truths, and creating ways of questioning long-untested orthodoxies.

It is not that firms do not learn from operating in the left loop of alignment and control, but some organisations evidently learn faster and more effectively than others. They seek out learning opportunities; they emphasise the virtues of curiosity and inquiry; they make a habit of questioning their assumptions;

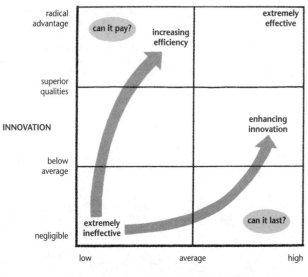

Combining efficiency and innovation

they purposefully frame bold new hypotheses; and they actively experiment with them. Even if a supine or control-besotted firm learns something from its accumulating everyday experiences, this clearly is not enough to gain it a noticeable competitive edge, since its competitors will be doing the same. In a quite well-run firm, the mere intensification of alignment and efficiency restricts its learning to that which will help it do better what it already does.

The right loop is not a mere option for any organisation that wants to lead, to win, to survive and prosper in good shape; it is a necessity. The message is simple: while efficiency and a control focus will keep you in the competitive game for a while, only fresh discoveries will enable you to win.

◈ The challenge of Discovery

DISCOVERY AND LEARNING are not synonyms, either for individuals or for organisations. Learning comes from two sources. It can come from moving knowledge around, such as teaching somebody something that is already known – though not known previously by the recipient. This is the foundation of "best practice", of "knowledge management" and of most examples of training. "Some people know more than us; let's find them and bottle their knowledge" is the motto. It is bringing the known to the unknowing.

The discovery process is more powerful than knowledge transfer or any form of "second-hand" learning. It involves creating as well as diffusing new knowledge. This is the domain of research, ideation, invention, experimentation and innovation. It goes well beyond the activity of simply rearranging existing information. The discoveries could be science-based breakthroughs, but they could equally be process-based, society-based or market-based.

The discovery process is founded on the notion that adults learn most from experiencing unfamiliar circumstances that nevertheless may have some potential relevance to their personal or organisational needs. The unfamiliar circumstances do not have to be threatening, for that can paralyse learning as fright takes hold. Nevertheless, discovery is experiential in taking people into an "unsafe", not wholly reassuring place – one where they feel slightly uncomfortable and which they would not have been likely to visit as part of their normal corporate lives. They are taken there to widen their perspectives; to become aroused to reconsider their assumptions; to reflect on their habitual limits to understanding;

and, with luck, to induce them to vow to expand their search for fresh insights.

The voyage of discovery takes you to marginal, edgy, unfamiliar places, which encourage participants to think anew and to reconsider their habitual assumptions. The more we learn about ourselves, the more we can view our own world with eyes freshened by these experiences; by departing from our familiarity, the more insightful and creative we will be back on our corporate terrain and the less will it resemble the kind of organisation that Gareth Morgan, author of *Images of Organisation*, used to characterise rhetorically as a "psychic prison". The first step in getting "out of the box" is to recognise that you are in one and the second is to discern what kind of box it is.

Too many organisations are fearful of such stimuli, or reject as unfocused even the idea of such stimuli. Instead, they feel that it is better, and safer, for their people to intensify their existing attention on narrow orthodoxies. This blinkered approach does not stop an organisation's managers claiming that they want their people to think imaginatively and radically, but then bemoaning the lack of genuinely novel ideas coming from them. A half-hearted approach to discovery is to visit straightforward business enterprises, as such visits rarely uplift and invigorate the boxed-in participants.

Many organisations have inhibiting pathologies; their leaders want control and find it difficult to let go, to even risk being playful; they are hobbled by defensive routines. Unwelcome information and jarring views are suppressed. In business, life can too often resemble a tramline, a single theory, an addiction to a "single path" of operation. "Mavericks beware" could be the unfortunate motto for all who enter the portals of an unimaginative firm.

One of the most depressing mantras of management has been the maxim, "no surprises". To which the obvious retort is: "What, not even good ones?" The whole approach of "no surprises" is so eviscerating that it can only have been dreamt up by financially entrapped control freaks. Its underlying rationale has some sense in that senior managers want to ensure that they are not embarrassed by being unaware of what is going on in their own organisation. Yet the whole ethos is negative. The assumption is that a surprise would have adverse effects, and that even if a surprise were positive, this would be evidence of a management control failure that would mark them down in the eyes of investors and commentators.

The skill in a discovery process is to engage people such that they are riveted by the experience in a way that motivates and galvanises them into undertaking personal and managerial initiatives inside their organisation. It widens their perspective, gives them heart to be more adventurous in their thinking, more holistic in their view of the world. What is striking is that the enthusiasm released by discovery experiences is sustained and that it tends to spread to others in the company, thus creating a multiplier effect. The learning leads to fruitful actions. And the dynamism does not seem to wane, but instead becomes embedded in these thoughtful organisations, far beyond the normal half-life of most development initiatives. Only grim organisations could fail to be uplifted by the catalytic effects of a good discovery process. It unlocks the latent curiosity of its people. It also brings out the best in younger, high-potential managers, and hence strengthens management teams and talent pools through the experiments and explorations they undertake once fired up by the discovery experience.

❧ The future and strength of the Discovery process

THE DISCOVERY PROCESS IS characterised by the following features:

- Those taking part choose to; they are not "managers sent on a course".
- Those who guide the process are catalysts and facilitators, not "teachers" or "instructors".
- Expertise is left at the door.
- Participants and facilitators are placed in contexts that challenge their expectations and assumptions.
- Unfamiliar locations and cultures are used to intensify curiosity and open-mindedness.
- Venues are chosen that are far removed from "classrooms", such as art galleries, photographic studios, temples and places of meditation, concert halls and rehearsal rooms, design museums, a billiard hall, a floating aquarium barge.
- Organisations are visited that work to different values and with different purposes, often having leaders motivated by a cause other than financial returns – particularly not-for-profit organisations, such as charities, government agencies, non-governmental organisations, social enterprises and arts organisations.
- These visits are arranged, but are unscripted.

Breakthrough learning involves – even requires – the crossing of different kinds of boundaries, whether intellectual, structural or emotional. Four particular types of boundary feature strongly in discovery activities:

- **Organisational and business boundaries – who participates in the events.** Learning is enhanced when there is a rich diversity of voices, perspectives and experiences in the room. Too many management courses limit themselves to a thin horizontal slice of the hierarchy. This is too comfortable and potentially limiting. Mixing levels, functions, business units and companies is much more potent.

- **Geographical and cultural boundaries – where the events are run.** Lecture theatres, "group rooms", hotel conference centres and corporate boardrooms are to be avoided. If participants feel as though they are in an office setting, or an educational establishment ("back at school"), they will play the role of manager or student obediently. The process must engage the real person. Roles, masks, egos and titles must be cast off. Going to an unfamiliar place can help achieve the necessary liberating effect.

- **Conceptual and disciplinary boundaries – what is the learning agenda of the programme.** The best way to sabotage a learning event is to come with "a solution", as it guarantees a closing of minds. Discovery depends on reframing whatever is the problem or the source of difficulty, perhaps by asking an unfamiliar or original set of questions, prompted by an eclectic mix of experiences, and thereby opening up the possibility of a radically new set of options. "Theories" often play the same deadening role as "solutions".

- **Methodological and pedagogical boundaries – how the learning agenda is delivered.** Lectures, PowerPoint presentations, handouts and all other "ready-mades" rarely help provoke the new thinking that discovery depends on. There should be no hard distinction between the roles of teacher and pupil, expert and novice, theoretician and practitioner. At different stages in a workshop, everyone should be permitted to play any of these roles. And it helps if the whole event has a coffee-break flavour, as in traditional educational settings it has been observed that the quality of the conversation picks up dramatically as everyone leaves the lecture theatre for a break.

The subversive nature of the Discovery process

MOST COMPANIES SEEK the wrong things from management-development programmes. Many adopt a highly instrumental, even philistine, view of the learning process. They want, and expect, the learning to serve the prevailing self-image of the organisation: its goals, its methods, its beliefs and its style. The hope, and expectation, is that those who go through a company-specific "training programme" will be better fitted to the party line, whatever it happens to be at the time.

However, learning cannot be constrained to a curriculum or to a cause or to a commitment. It sets its own direction. By definition, it is unpredictable and uncontrollable. This is why it is so powerful. It contains surprises.

All too often companies want business schools to "professionalise" their managers, as though there were a body of knowledge that stands to management as physics stands to engineering. As a result, the typical corporate brief to which business schools are invited to respond, framed inevitably in terms of learning objectives and measures of success, pushes the design of the programme to the left-hand side of the list of desiderata below. By contrast, the discovery process is designed explicitly to operate on the right-hand side.

what is needed is NOT ...	BUT ...
more knowledge	the courage and confidence to apply what we already know
the latest theories	the chance to make sense of our own unique experiences
stronger alignment	the right to question assumptions and challenge dogma
broader consensus	the obligation to honour and engage with the voices of dissent
tighter controls	the curiosity to explore and experiment with alternative options
more measures	the maturity to exercise judgment
a clearer vision	the courage to live closer to the edge of chaos and emergence
new initiatives	the self-discipline to do fewer, braver things
greater activity	the wisdom to live less frenetically and more reflectively
stronger leadership	the enlightenment to take responsibility for our own choices

The assumptions that underpin the discovery process in management education

The Discovery process depends on an open and subjective agenda

···

."And the end of all our exploring
Will be to arrive where we started
And know the place for the first time."

T.S. Eliot

Setting expectations

It is easy to over-prepare for a learning session. The art is to live the experience "in the present". Attempts to predict the nature, the meaning, or the outcome of the experience serve only to strengthen intellectual and emotional defences. It is better to focus on the skills of productive conversation, the importance (and difficulty) of attending to what others are saying and meaning; the principles of appreciative inquiry; or conversational gambits that help promote deeper dialogue. In other words, the approach should be to dwell lightly on the process of effective engagement and not to try to anticipate the meaning of the experience. Above all, emphasis should be put on the power of simply noticing things – both in the external world and in our own reactions to what we see – with participants urged to suspend judgment and simply attend to what is around them.

Thinking ahead

Participants should be asked what barriers could inhibit their learning from these experiences; advised to ask themselves what they might learn from the visits; reminded that the more intelligent the questions they ask, the more they will learn, as they seek to understand, not to judge, by asking depersonalised questions. A well-designed discovery process is a tribute to the importance of conversation.

Navigating the journey

The fixed points are few – essentially no more than start and finish times. The rest is open to improvisation and serendipity. Participants must be encouraged to take full responsibility for what happens and for what learning they get out of the sessions. It is their agenda and it is for them to set it and then honour it. In keeping with this principle, the role of the facilitator involves little more than being the group's timekeeper (relieving participants of logistical anxieties) and conscience (holding them to their own self-set task). The role of keeping a careful record of each session and every discussion, including taking photographs and making videos, is for the participants to allocate.

Making sense of the journey

It is worth spending almost as much time reflecting on the sessions as making them. A day's worth of first-hand experiences demands at least a morning's worth of sense-making. It is illuminating to realise how different people extract different meanings from the same, shared experience. This variety of interpretations needs to be captured and codified. The task of "making sense" includes honouring the sheer diversity of people's "take" on the same experience. The obligation to share your learning with others, both within your team and across the group as a whole, calls for a special skill that might be called "storytelling". The tendency of many executives would be to distil their thoughts and reactions into a set of bullet points on a slide – and then simply to play back this sequence of points. But such a presentation will give little flavour of the real experience and even less indication of its emotional, moral and intellectual significance to the author. Much more meaning can be obtained if participants re-create the experience by means of a short play, or a collage of images, or a story in the form of a fable, with everyone in the group, whether or not they were first-hand witnesses of that experience, feeling as though they were present.

Telling stories

Mike Placko, founder of The Discovery Practice™, noticed that the stories that participants tell typically conform to one of three basic plots:

- **Transformation stories** – "I used to believe that ... then I had the experience of ... and learned that ... and now I view the world differently."
- **Revelation stories** – "I had no idea that ... it never occurred to me that ... and now these new notions, opportunities and perspectives ... influence the way I think about ..."
- **Confirmation stories** – "I have been thinking, believing, acting in certain ways ... and now I have had the experience of ... I find that my views have been reinforced, confirmed."

Putting the experience to work

Participants are usually keen to turn their newly found energy and ideas into practical solutions for their business. After the sessions, they reflect on what they have seen and learned (often being surprised at how differently individuals can interpret the same visits, and how much that leads to deep debates about issues and experiences). Two aspects of the experiences emerge: first, reflections about themselves and how they usually work; and second, what this could mean for their own organisation and for their own part in it.

Decentering

To build upon this argument, participants are invited to reappraise their own organisation by observing it through the eyes of another. We call this the "inside-out exercise". "Please describe", participants are asked, "what the people you have just visited would say if, in return, they visited your company." Participants are often surprised at how differently their own organisation appears when they observe it through fresh eyes. They see that what are widely held management orthodoxies are just assumptions, which may or may not be valid. Participants become more aware that some things they have taken for granted are not universally held or experienced; that there are choices. They see that there are different ways of approaching things, thinking about things, valuing things; that more possibilities exist; and that their own actions, and the fortunes of their own organisation, might be improved by their acting in a more liberated, less conformist fashion.

The important flavour of unpredictability and ambiguity

"Discover remarkable people doing remarkable things in remarkable ways – scratch the ordinary all around us and you will find the extraordinary." **Mike Placko**

THE DISCOVERY PROCESS involves participants in making an open-minded approach to organisations that are doing unusual things in unusual ways.

Examples might include the following:

● A visit to a well-run Amsterdam "coffee shop", which is a cannabis/marijuana retailer, and finding that its owners include MBAs; that the restrictions on stock involve its having an extremely efficient just-in-time delivery system; that its activities are in a highly uncertain demi-monde since they are not illegal but they are not legal either, and that in consequence the coffee-shop managers liaise amicably but informally with the local residential community, the police and the local authorities; that its typical clients are professionals, not drug-sodden crazies; and that its busiest period is the early evening when its architect and lawyer clients are relaxing after work. All these features might be a surprise. They are seen as relevant but startling revelations. Not only that: the coffee-shop business is also engaged in genetic research and plant growing to improve the quality and consistency of the several varieties of the product (which is one reason why soft drugs have been getting steadily stronger), and its managers have the belief, possibly erroneous, that major tobacco companies are readying themselves for the legalisation of soft drugs and have bought up large tracts of land in Mexico for that eventuality.

- A visit to a particularly crime-ridden and deprived area of a North American city where reformed criminals – some of whom have served many years in penitentiaries for crimes of extreme violence – have committed themselves to helping vulnerable youngsters to avoid their own earlier fate and dissuade them from slipping into a life of crime.

- Visits involving artistic activities, meeting the head of a ballet company, a leading museum, or an orchestra conductor, all of whom create experiences which entail the effective co-ordination of egotistical experts – rather like managing creative teams in an advertising agency, or academics in a business school, or research scientists in a laboratory.

Visits made as part of the discovery process could open participants' eyes to a stunningly different retirement village, or a community under ethnic siege, a hospital for terminally ill children, a workshop for the mentally and physically handicapped, or an inner-city charity that, like many public services, can only fulfil its mission by serving anyone who wants what it offers, unlike a commercial firm that can choose which customers to serve and which to ignore.

The most compelling and influential visits for participants from commercial organisations are not those that are directly connected to business – which are often called "industrial tourism" – but those that focus on social innovation, for these take the participants out of their normal context and are more challenging and memorable. It helps if the experience is personally inspiring. For this to happen, participants must open themselves to the views, experiences and beliefs of those they visit. It is about crossing boundaries, which, in a globalising world, is what many executives now need to do.

Discovery is a close cousin of action learning, pioneered by Reg Revans, a management scholar. Yet it does have one significant difference. Where action learning uses self-chosen teams ("comrades in adversity" as Revans called them) to find creative ways of solving an organisational problem, discovery does not start with a given business objective. Instead it seeks to stimulate fresh insights that are then used to find business issues to tackle. Discovery emphasises the value of immersing executives in unfamiliar organisations that are achieving extraordinary results in unusual ways, often through the skill and energy of a remarkable leader. Through dialogue, executives are encouraged to make sense of their cognitive and emotional experience of interacting with these individuals and their organisations. In doing so, participants find themselves reframing and reformulating their own mental models and then using these insights to reappraise their habits and perspectives. In effect, it becomes a journey of self-discovery.

Prudential and the potency of live testing

Prudential is a multinational financial services company. Over the past few years, ten one-week discovery programmes have been designed and delivered for groups of 20 executives at a time, drawn from around the world. The locations of these workshops have been San Francisco, Singapore, Boston, Amsterdam, Los Angeles, Austin (Texas), Hong Kong, Washington, DC, and Philadelphia.

To give a flavour of the kinds of visits that were made in these cities, some of the organisations visited by Prudential executives, in groups of 5–7 participants, are as follows.

San Francisco:

- Valley Venturing: a venture capital company in Silicon Valley
- Women.com: a portal devoted to feminine issues and lifestyles
- Frye's: an electronics superstore

- Sierra Club: an environmental advocacy group
- Habitat for Humanity: a housing association for the underprivileged
- Big Brothers Big Sisters: a child mentoring organisation
- Double Twist: a genomics company dealing with pre-disposition testing
- Cisco Internet Solutions: the department responsible for business innovation
- Delancey Street Foundation: a community drug-rehabilitation centre
- YMCA: a charity supporting teenagers in after-school hours
- Stanford Business Entrepreneurship Programme: a business school course designed to build entrepreneurs

Boston:

- Lassell College: a university and residential home for senior citizens
- The Shapiro Clinical Centre: new practices in health care
- The Boston Police Department: new models of community policing
- The Emergency Shelter Commission: caring for the homeless
- The Boston Living Centre: caring for those with HIV/AIDS
- The Cambridge Zen Centre: the spiritual dimension in today's world
- Communispace: using technology to build virtual communities
- Ella Baker House: caring for troubled youth in the community

Inspired by these visits – and others in the same vein in the other cities – 34 experiments were designed, with titles such as latent assets, group information exchange, testing attitudes, jester, spread lending, InPRUbator, Me to the Power of U, customer passions, Pru University, work-life balance, team challenge and human capital.

These experiments can be grouped into six broad categories:

- Knowledge management
- The power of the group
- Innovation
- Networks/relationships
- Customer focus
- The company and the individual

Below, the experiments of two different teams, one in Hong Kong and the other in Austin, Texas, illustrate some typical outcomes of the discovery process.

In Hong Kong, one team was inspired by a visit to a farm in the New Territories, where they discovered that men and women well into their 80s were still working the land. In conversation with them, they reflected on the bizarre Western notion of "retirement" and how much of the Prudential product portfolio – particularly pension plans and health plans – was dependent on the continuity of retirement as a deep-seated habit, or orthodoxy, of advanced Western economies. Here they were confronted by the realisation that perhaps retirement was a temporary aberration and that the West too would soon lapse back into lifelong work.

In the light of these meditations, they designed an experiment to test the notion of a health-insurance plan with premiums based on the policyholder adhering to a particular fitness regime. In other words, you "proactively" set the price of your policy – if you exercise hard, the premiums will come down, and vice versa. This idea, which tested well, is now part of one of Prudential's new products. It reflects a growing recognition that responsibility for managing their old age is going to fall increasingly on individual citizens – and that the state's role is certain to decline in importance.

In Austin, a team was impressed by the self-reliance, optimism and independence of thought of many of the social entrepreneurs they met, even under conditions of real difficulty and hardship.

They reflected that, in their own commercial world, as soon as a difficulty arose, consultants would be called in. From this insight, they proposed an experiment to test whether an internal team, acting as consultants, could come up with the same quality of recommendations as an external team.

Jonathan Bloomer, the chief executive at the time, who sat in on the presentations of all the experiments coming out of the discovery programme, immediately saw an opportunity to test this idea, called "Team Challenge". Regulations in the UK had just been changed to allow insurance companies, such as Prudential, to acquire independent financial advisers (IFAs). Previously, this had been thought to introduce a conflict of interest. Normally, the first reaction to such a change in the law would be to commission consultants to present the options and recommend a course of action. This time, an internal team from across the world was assembled, brought to London, provided with office space and secretarial support, and given six weeks to come up with a report, including advice on how the company should respond, and present their findings to the board. The result was a triumph. The report was judged to have been excellent, the young team members had had a powerful learning experience, and the business was well served by the quality of advice given.

BG Group and the power of heretical thinking

One of the most dramatic examples of the power of the discovery method to redirect a company's strategy and unlock hidden potential featured BG Group, a British-based global energy company. A medium-sized player in 2004, based originally on the privatised assets of British Gas, a government-owned business, BG had grown its asset base since privatisation well beyond the North Sea assets that had established British Gas as a major supplier of gas. During the 1990s, BG had acquired gas fields in Egypt, Tunisia, Italy, Kazakhstan, Trinidad and elsewhere to the point where its North Sea assets represented a small and diminishing portion of its assets.

During a discovery workshop involving members of the North Sea asset-management team, a challenge was made: to identify one of the most important unspoken assumptions of their business and to explore the consequences of its not being true. There were to be no constraints on their imagination. The younger members of the team quickly isolated two critical assumptions:

- First, that the North Sea gas fields were a depleting asset, evidenced particularly by the fact that most of the major oil and gas companies were already moving their focus away from the North Sea and towards the exciting new areas.
- Second, that BG's North Sea business should be managed as a cash cow, with its profits being used to cross-subsidise exploration activities in these newer areas. Any other strategy, particularly a self-serving strategy, would be interpreted as disloyal and harmful to the prosperity of the company as a whole.

On the basis of these two heresies, they put forward an enthusiastic case, buttressed by an idiosyncratic but ingenious interpretation of the geology of the region, to continue prospecting in the North Sea – and, by implication, treat the business as anything but a cash cow.

As soon as these heresies were uttered, and despite the call that nothing was off-limits, the managing director of the North Sea business, a talented man who had bravely put himself and his team forward for the first event but who was now distinctly worried by the turn of events, admonished his young team for going too far, for being immature and for jeopardising the serious purpose of the workshop. He was adamant that they abandon this line of thinking and choose instead a heresy that "demonstrated responsibility and made clear business sense". The young managers were dismayed and felt dispirited, but they adjusted their approach and chose to challenge less sacrosanct orthodoxies of the business.

A few months later, the managing director was promoted to a different part of the business and a new managing director, fresh from managing the company's Egyptian assets, took over the North Sea business. Recognising rather low levels of morale within his team, he asked them where they saw the future of the business. This was their chance to try out their former heresy on their new boss. He was intrigued. Further geophysical studies were commissioned. Permission from the board to drill in the North Sea was gained. An extension to the Buzzard field was discovered, one of the more important gas finds of the decade.

Such is the power, on occasion, of heretical thinking. Without the context of "discovery visits" designed to whet the appetite for heretical thinking, and without the permission to "think the unthinkable" in the context of a one-week workshop, it is not self-evident that BG would have had the time, the courage or the opportunity to build such a powerful case for testing its North Sea assumptions and thereby boost massively its market value.

A feature of the series of discovery events designed for BG was an emphasis on visits to inspiring and effective voluntary organisations. One impact of these visits across all the groups of managers who made them was a growing recognition of the power vested in communities of activists to make a positive difference. They also served to highlight the importance of a passionate commitment to a cause, of a task that truly taxes one's abilities, and of an organisation that is worthy of one's loyalty.

A large part of BG's success since privatisation in the mid-1980s had been its hard-driving performance management system, a classic example of the control loop being applied in a particularly single-minded way. But by 2000, it was increasingly felt that the company was relying too much on only one method of performance delivery. Reviewing the state of the business in 2003, Sir Frank Chapman, the CEO, framed the idea of what he chose to call "BG Society". He left the definition of his notion purposefully vague, so as to inspire his people to "discover" what it could come to mean and what business benefits it could deliver. But clearly he saw "BG Society" as complementary to the rather instrumentalist culture of the organisation. He was keen to promote the virtues of a civil society within his own organisation, he was acknowledging the importance of the "social capital" of the company, and he was looking for ways of strengthening the bonds of allegiance, mutuality and trust among his people. Under this broad rubric of "BG Society", a large number of organisation-strengthening and community-building initiatives have been taken.

Under the leadership of Malcolm Tulloch, the BG executive responsible for organisational development and learning, the discovery programmes have supported his conviction that skills of dialogue are the distinctive capability that most dramatically differentiates a professional culture such as that of BG. Working in the Chris Argyris tradition of "action science" and the Bill Torbert tradition of "action inquiry", Tulloch uses the model of productive conversation not only to enhance the value of the discovery visits themselves, but also to make collective sense of these experiences and then to work together to design experiments that are ingenious and fruitful. Out of these experiences has emerged a strong commitment to the development of a coaching culture.

Danone and one step on the mountain

Danone is a multinational food-products company based in France. Members of the executive board (COMEX) visited Treehouse, a school for severely autistic children in North London, where the instruction is entirely one-on-one and based on a method of instruction known as applied behavioural analysis. There were 50 teachers responsible for the education of roughly the same number of children. For six hours a day, individual children are taught by a single specially trained teacher – and this teacher works with the same child over at least a whole school year (40 weeks or so).

Each executive spent 30 minutes observing a teaching session and then 15 minutes discussing it with the instructor. What struck the executives were the painfully slow progress of the learning and the inordinately patient attention of the teacher. Seemingly trivial achievements following hours (even days) of teaching were greeted by everyone as a huge step worth celebrating. One of the teachers described the overall mission of the school as "a mountain" – and the summit of the mountain represented a child sufficiently educated by the school to be able to lead an independent life by the time he or she left. Any small step on the journey to the summit was a source of pride.

Franck Riboud, chairman and CEO of Danone, speaking later to a group of his senior managers, said how moved he had been by the analogy of the journey to the summit. He confessed that, by comparison with Treehouse, Danone did not have a clear picture of the mountain it was attempting to climb; nor did it have a culture that measured and celebrated every step on the journey. He suggested that perhaps a mountain worthy of Danone's skills and resources would be to nourish the undernourished of the world, and that the processes of the company should be designed to work towards achieving this. Indeed, since 2005, Danone has launched many social initiatives around the world and has pioneered a hybrid business model combining social enterprise and business acumen.

The effect of the Treehouse experience has been that – in a spirit of exploration and enterprise, and with a feeling that "anything is possible", and a strong "can do" attitude – executives from Danone have made visits to a wide variety of organisations in Amsterdam chosen to represent novel and innovative ways of creating value; they included an art school for disabled adults, a restaurant that grows its own produce, a university dedicated wholly to high-level sporting achievement and an urban monastery in the red-light district.

These experiences have inspired a number of experiments focused on various ways of enhancing and accelerating Danone's innovation activities, and challenging Danone's favoured "fast second" strategy, as exemplified by its success with Actimel in the slipstream of Yakult's invention of a new dairy category. The table overleaf illustrates the nature of the ideas that the executives involved in the Amsterdam visits came up with.

chosen themes of the experiments	strengthening the innovation processes in Danone	growing a new service business in Danone	enhancing organisational learning within Danone	adding an incubator to the structure of Danone
synergies to be captured	working across functional boundaries, particularly R&D and marketing	working across activity boundaries, particularly products and services	working across geographical boundaries, particularly Asia and Europe	working across business boundaries into "white space opportunities"
locus of change	Danone's processes	Danone's business model	Danone's corporate model	Danone's structure
concept of value	managing against the grain of the structure	deepening and broadening the customer relationship	exchanging leading internal practices	growing Danone's "innovation premium" in the capital markets

The Danone "Leading Edge Programme": four experimental outcomes

◕ Emotional engagement is crucial

THE MAIN BENEFITS that come out of the discovery process are as follows.

A jolt to the system

Learning begins with wonder; but typically the palates of adults have become so jaded that they rarely experience awe, astonishment or genuine wonder. Hence the importance of experiences that are sufficiently new and unfamiliar to engage people at a visceral level. Only in a state of imbalance would real learning seem to be possible.

A stronger dose of reality

The greatest teacher is the raw experience of living. And the way to intensify or accelerate people's experience of life is to purposefully immerse them in an unfamiliar environment where there are few "intellectual handholds". The inherent human need to make sense of any new experience works to ensure that new meanings are made. The mind remodels itself on this new world – and this is learning.

Ronald Heifetz, co-founder of the Centre for Public Leadership at the John F. Kennedy School of Government, Harvard University, and of Cambridge Leadership Associates, distinguishes between technical and adaptive mental work when we move into an unfamiliar world. The technical response is to "force-fit" the world to the contours of our pre-existing intellectual framework. Perceptively, we filter out those elements of the new experience that are inconsistent or unexpected. This, of course, is particularly disabling if learning is the main purpose. By contrast, the adaptive response is to pay particular attention to that which is new and to put our creative energy into adjusting our mental models to take into account (and thereby to account for) the entire "bandwidth" of the experience.

Enhanced self-awareness

These experiences are as much journeys of self-discovery as explorations of other worlds. Confronted with the unfamiliar, we come face-to-face with our own preconceptions and biases. By identifying and exposing our tacit assumptions, we gain greater control of our belief system and, indeed, our identity. Peter Senge, author of *The Fifth Discipline*, has given the name "personal mastery" to this enhanced sense of self.

Stimulus to the imagination

Without necessarily knowing it, we are held back by the poverty of our imagination and the paucity of our invented options. In solving business problems, we typically consider far too narrow a range of alternatives. Travel helps to remind us that the scope for innovation is far broader and richer than we sometimes assume. It arouses our curiosity and takes off the blinkers.

Creative outpouring of ideas

The intensity of the inputs delivered by a discovery experience tends to be matched by the ingenuity of the ideas and initiatives emanating from the experience. Witnessing first-hand the energy and commitment of others, we find ourselves emulating their self-belief and self-confidence. We feel renewed – and this shows up as entrepreneurial zest. It is interesting that the learning engendered by these journeys is less likely to be the transfer of concrete knowledge through the benchmarking of particular processes or practices, and more likely to be the contagious quality of particular people's attitudes, personalities and perspectives.

Recognition of our fallibility

We are beset by all manner of illusions and delusions. Often, we are prisoners of our own (limited) experiences. We need to create situations and encounters that bring these forms of error into the open, make them subject to debate and render them dispensable.

Diminution of perceived risk

Our plans and projects are often dominated by an exaggerated sense of the risk of error. It is the precision of our fears and anxieties that crowds out the vagueness of our hopes and dreams. Discovery can enhance our sense of optimism and self-confidence.

An experimental mindset

The enthusiasm engendered by discovery translates into a strong desire to try out new things and to experiment with different ways of working. The intent is not necessarily to roll out the latest panacea across the whole organisation, but rather to put in place a number of small, local experiments designed to test a variety of newly formulated hypotheses. Discovery promotes a trial-and-error method of working and learning.

Group bonding

Journeys of exploration, particularly visits to voluntary organisations working with disadvantaged clients and communities, bring out the social instinct in groups. A team spirit develops and a desire to collaborate in the pursuit of shared goals is a natural outcome. When, with colleagues, we show our emotions and share our feelings, our common humanity shows through and we find ourselves communicating in a more open, sincere and candid manner. These moments of trust, once experienced, are never forgotten. They are the building blocks of "social capital formation" within the firm.

Final words

THIS HAS BEEN A BOOK for rational optimists. Our ideas are intended for managers who have not lost their idealism, and we hope that we have offered useful insights, interpretations, models, motives and methods for anyone who has aspirations to lead.

We hope that we have made a dent in many of the tired and cynical assumptions that underpin the organisational routines and rituals that kill enthusiasm at work and that act as a drag on the natural inventiveness and ingenuity of employees. Our clear intention is to change the way in which modern organisations define their ends and design their means. We hope that we have made a compelling case for the reinvention of management and the redesign of the working environment.

Our underlying and fervent belief is that the potent blend of scientific thinking and market institutions that increasingly characterises the open societies of the world today, is the dynamic that will propel the global economy to ever-increasing levels of human achievement, prosperity and personal fulfilment.

Acknowledgements

::

OUR GOOD FORTUNE is to have had the opportunity to work creatively and collaboratively with senior teams in hundreds of executive workshops that we have designed and delivered, many of them at London Business School. To these many managers we owe a huge debt of gratitude – for their energy, their imagination and their optimism.

During these workshops, we have interacted with managers to imagine alternative futures, to diagnose performance bottlenecks, to open minds to new options, to challenge accepted practice, to invent new ways of working and to draw up plans for change. In the vigour of these creative, often chaotic conversations, we began to discern patterns, to notice what worked or did not work, and to distil a small number of critical concepts and helpful stratagems that together form the foundations of this book. We owe much to the managers from whom we have learned and to the organisations with which we have tested our evolving ideas.

Our notion of asymmetric beliefs as the foundation of organisational success – the idea that winning involves the discovery of uncommon sense and the renunciation of common nonsense – was developed over the course of our long-standing relationships with the senior management teams at Orange, Rolls-Royce, Smith & Nephew, Rio Tinto, Freshfields Bruckhaus Deringer and Deutsche Bank.

The discovery method of experiential learning – essentially the week-long immersion of business teams in an "alien culture" – originated with a groundbreaking series of workshops, co-designed with Mike Placko, the founder of the Discovery Practice™, for Prudential, launched in 2000 and held in 12 cities over the succeeding 10 years. The idea proved to be so powerful that we extended and refined the idea in our work for BG Group, Danone, Starwood and Volvo.

Our frustration with managerialism – the recognition that most firms today can be hamstrung by organisational assumptions, routines and rituals that make sense only in the context of 19th-century industrial habits – found a home in the Management Innovation Lab at London Business School, founded by Gary Hamel and Julian Birkinshaw. It was in this congenial and inspirational setting that we developed our "post-managerialist" model of organisation.

The idea that experimentation is the antidote to organisational dogma has become the hallmark of our teaching practice. In many companies, but particularly in our work with Roche, we have seen truly extraordinary insights emerge from the live testing of bold hypotheses formulated by teams of managers.

The radical nature of our work has only been possible because of the courage and creativity of the CEOs who have sponsored our workshops, in particular Tom Albanese, Jonathan Bloomer, Sir Frank Chapman, Sir Chris O'Donnell, Franck Riboud, Sir John Rose, Anthony Salz and Hans Snook.

We are also indebted to the HR directors and heads of learning and development who became our personal clients, in particular Barry Bloch, Thierry Bonetto, Clare Chandler, Pascal Desbourdes, Eamonn Eaton, Peter Hessey, Tim Hornblow, Jane Kibby, Franck Mougin, John Rivers, Lynne Rutherford, Tony Schneider, Malcolm Tulloch and Paul Williams.

With our choice of career, we were particularly lucky. Our academic careers began not long after Europe had founded its first business schools. How fortuitous this was. We were in on the ground floor, so to speak, helping to lay the foundations for a new curriculum of praxis, for new combinations of disciplines, for new methods of learning and for non-traditional styles of research. It was a time of intellectual ferment. We benefited from the companionship and wisdom of many of the pioneers who led this revolution: Sir James Ball, Andrew Ehrenberg, Sir Douglas Hague, Charles Handy, Tom Lupton, Grigor McClelland, John Morris, Enid Mumford, Derek Pugh, Denis Pym, Reg Revans, Harold Rose, Kenneth Simmonds, Sir Roland Smith, John Stopford and Douglas Wood.

Over the past 15 years, our intellectual debt has been to the succeeding generation of business school colleagues with whom we have worked closely and by whom we have been encouraged and inspired: Patrick Barwise, Julie Brennan, René Carayol, Yves Doz, Paul Evans, Mary Farebrother, Jane Farran, Rob Goffee, Peter Gorley, Lynda Gratton, Ian Hardie, Gay Haskins, Terry Hill, Veronica Hope-Hailey, Dominic Houlder, John Hunt, Gareth Jones, Dana Kaminstein, Richard Lewis, Sir Andrew Likierman, Costas Markides, Alan Matcham, Jens Meyer, Henry Mintzberg, Kate Ng, Nigel Nicholson, Eddie Obeng, John Quelch, Tom Robertson, Jose Santos, Fons Trompenaars, Kim Warren, Bill Weinstein, David Weir, Robin Wensley, Paul Willman and Sharon Wilson.

We are very grateful to Simon Brown and Helen Duguid for reading and improving the manuscript.

Our editor at Profile Books, Stephen Brough, and our copy-editor, Penny Williams, both deserve huge credit for seeing the book to press, always with immense encouragement and wise advice. Lastly, to Cherry Goddard, we owe our special thanks for her beautiful illustrations.

Jules Goddard: jgoddard@dial.pipex.com

Tony Eccles: tonyjeccles@gmail.com